FAMOUS IN TAMIL NADU

CW00536786

Dr. Ramesh Pokhriyal 'Nishank'

DIAMOND BOOKS

www.diamondbook.in

All rights are reserved. No part of this publication may be reproduced, stored in a retrieval system or transmitted in any form or by any means, electronic, mechanical, photocopying, recording or otherwise, without the prior permission of the copyright holder.

© Author

Publisher	:	**Diamond Pocket Books (P) Ltd.**
		X-30, Okhla Industrial Area, Phase-II
		New Delhi-110020
Phone	:	011-40712200
E-mail	:	sales@dpb.in
Website	:	www.dpb.in
Edition	:	2023
Printed by	:	**Mercury Communication Services, Delhi**

Famous Temples in Tamil Nadu
Author : *Dr. Ramesh Pokhriyal 'Nishank'*

CONTENTS

INTRODUCTION

The temples of South India, especially of Tamil Nadu, are known for their grandeur in size, architectural styles and iconographical features. The temples portray the rich past of the region in terms of the history and culture. Temple towns, which are a major characteristic of the Tamil provinces, house temples of massive proportions. Belonging to the Dravidian style of architecture, the temples of Tamil Nadu range from modest sized temples to very large ones of high artistic merit. The temples have gone through a long process of evolution from the Sangam age to late medieval times. The Sangam age saw much encouragement being extended to several forms of art. Initially, the works of art and architecture were made of perishable materials, but, in course of time, stone came in for extensive applications. In fact, in as far as Indian architecture is concerned, the shift to stone, a more lasting material has been a significant step in the evolution of architecture in India. Temples were patronised by the royalty, nobility, landlords, wealthy merchants, guilds as well as lay devotees, including those of lower castes and classes. Such acts of patronage contributed to the expansion of temple complexes with its series of pillared halls (mandapams), enclosures (praharas) and gateways (gopuras), and a horizontal expansion of the temples, creating physical and religious space for the complex society and economy that developed in Tamil Nadu during the medieval period.

Moreover, construction of temples was looked upon as not only a sacred act but also an act of merit. Architects were even honoured by the State. Kings who appreciated art encouraged it and many of them were themselves the connoisseurs of art. The Pallava king Mahendravarman I, for example, is said to have been learned in the art of painting, sculpture, literature and engineering, and was known as a tiger among artists. As a mark of encouragement, several grants were made to shrines, besides the rulers, by the members of the royal family, including queens and princesses. Royal patronage was important in the case of specific shrines and reflected the close relationship that the kings sought to establish with certain deities and temples. A large number of inscriptions point to donations made to temples in the form of land, ornaments, constructions, pujas, fairs, festivals and other forms of grants. Guilds, both of craftsmen and merchants, contributed to the construction and maintenance of temples as well as celebration of festivals. Inscriptions, giving details of donations were issued by kings in temples which fell within their own territory or even sometimes located in the regions of other kingdoms. To this day, giving donations to temples, and contributing towards the 'Kumbabhishegam' (consecration ceremony, aimed at uniting the mystic powers of the temple), are held in high esteem in Tamil Nadu and finding a mention in the temple plaques is considered an honour.

With large number of donations pouring in, temples became rich institutions and nuclei of religious, social and economic activities. Temples provided employment to large numbers, including priests, dancing girls, artisans and other functionaries. Besides, they also functioned as banks and educational institutions, as in most instances. Pathashalas were, and are still, attached to several of the temples. Festivals and fairs of the temples, which were a feature of a large number of temples, had socio-religious and economic significance, attracting people from far and wide.

Famous Temples in Tamil Nadu

Architectural Historians subdivide the period of Dravidian Architectural growth into Pallava, Chola, Pandiya, Vijayanagara and Nayakkar Periods. The era of temple building activity commenced with the rise of Pallavas to power in the later half of sixth century AD. It is believed that the Southern or Dravidian architectural style of building was initiated by the Pallavas who held sway till the ninth century AD over an extensive region in Southern India. A phase of intense architectural activity, both with rock-cut and structural designs, was witnessed. The free standing monolithic rathas, the rock-cut mandapams and temples of majestic proportions, located within large Praharas, are the best representations of the Pallava style, seen at Mahabalipuram and Kanchipuram.

The foundations of the Dravidian School laid by the Pallavas flowered under the Cholas. They are considered prolific temple builders and, therefore, the age of the Cholas is called the golden age of Dravidian architecture. Remarkable also are Chola contributions to metal sculptures as seen in the bronze sculptures of Siva Nataraja, the Cosmic Dancer and of Vishnu and Lakshmi. The temples, under Cholas, were also embellished with captivating iconography, which has been said to have provided to the architecture, an embellishment that gave rhythm and harmony. A new trend in Dravidian architecture took shape under the Pandiyas who rose to power with the decline of the Chola power. Additional structures to the existing temples, tall Praharas and towering gopurams, came to be added which saw the expansion of the temple complexes.

Under the patronage of the Vijayanagara Empire, with the extension of Imperial rule over vast tracts of the south, architectural activity was undertaken on an extensive scale. Architectural traditions of the earlier periods provided the necessary back-drop for further growth of the Dravidian Style of architecture. With the extension of temple complex with tall praharas and gopuras, popularly known as Rayagopurams as well as several additional structures like the Amman Koil, and a number of open pillared mandapams came into being, all indicative of increased ecclesiastical activities during the period. Characteristic of the style was also the variety of pillars as well as the human, animal and mythical yali were chiselled out of solid stone and fixed to the shafts of the pillars.

With the emergence of the Nayakas, as the successors of the Vijayanagara Empire, royal patronage to temples continued. In the Tamil provinces, the contribution of the Nayakas of Madurai has been the most significant. The lavish growth of architecture could be seen in the buildings of several shrines and structures within the vast temple complexes, including imposing mahadwaras and gopurams. This phase also saw an increasing number of uthsavams and ceremonies celebrated in the temples.

In many of the large temples of South India, will be seen a wooden chariot located in an isolated corner of the temple complex. The chariot or ratha, a miniature model of the temple shrine is used for parading the processional idols or uthsavamurtis. The wooden chariots are richly decorated with figures of divine and semi-divine beings, narrative friezes, floral designs, animal figures as well as mythical animals. The ceremonial procession is usually carried through the car streets or rathaveedhis during the temple festivals. On the day of the rathothsava, the idols of the deities are given a holy bath or Thirumanjanam and adorned with silk garments, ornaments and flowers.

1. SRI KANCHI KAMAKSHI AMMAN TEMPLE

In this magnificent temple, the Goddess Kamakshi prevails in the form of Shakti. The temple is one of the 51 Shakti Peethas across the country. The goddess's residing place in Kanchi is called as "Nabisthana Ottiyana Peetam". This temple is of unconfirmed antiquity. The temple was most probably built between 5th century BCE and 8th century AD, by the pallava kings whose capital was Kanchipuram.

The temple is spread over five acres of land and has four entrance points. From the outside, the spire of the temple, covered in Gold, is clearly visible. At the main entrance of the temple, one finds Mahisasura Mardini on the right side, Kalabhairava on the left side and a massive Dwajasthambam at the very center. The idol of Lord Vinayaka comes before darshan of the Goddess Kamakshi. On the outer prakaram of the temple, the main deity of Goddess Kamakshi is surrounded by the deities of Saraswathi, Annapoorna, Ayyappa and Adi Shankaracharya. The hundred pillared hall of the temple or the Dhwajaarohana Mandapam is situated on the outer Prakaram of the temple. The shrines of Soundaryalakshmi and Arthanareeswar are also situated within the Kamakshi Amman temple. Panch Ganga is the main tank of the temple. Another deity, that is worshipped in the temple, is the Arupa Lakshmi. The Kumkum archana is, in fact, devoted to Arupa Lakshmi, though it is offered to Goddess Kamakshi. There is a Srichakra Yantra (Shri Kamakoti Peetam) established by Jagadguru Sri Aadishankaracharya in front of the Goddess deity.

Kanchi is also called as Satyavrita Kshetra. Legends have it that the Goddess worshipped Lord Siva by creating a mud idol in Kanchi. At that moment, Lord Siva incarnated as Kamba River with high tides to test the worship of the goddess, the goddess grasped the idol closely with her two hands from eroding in the tides. This prevented the idol from getting eroded in the floods. The goddess also performed Pooja by sitting in a needle tip surrounded by "Panchakagni" (surrounded by 5 fires) to free herself from the interest of livelihood. The Lord Shiva was pleased by the goddess's devotion, appeared before her and married the goddess.

Though there are many Shiva temples in the city, the only temple to have the sanctorum of the goddess is the Sri Kamakshi Amman Temple. There are also eight other Shakti goddesses surrounding the temple.

The place where goddess resides is "Gayatri Mandapam". The goddess lives in temple in 3 forms. The forms are that of Sri Kamakshi, Sri Bilahasam and Sri Chakram. The goddess is in a sitting posture of "Padmasana". The goddess contains Pasa, Angusa, Pushpabana and Sugarcane in her forehands.

The mythology of Daksha yaga and Sati's self-immolation is the main theme in the origin of Shakti Peethas. Shakti Peethas are the divine temples of Adiparashakti. The sanctum houses the image of Kamakshi in seated posture and is flanked by the trinity of Shiva, Vishnu, and Brahma. There are smaller shrines of Bangaru Kamakshi, Adi Shankara and Maha Saraswathi around the sanctum. The temple sanctorum consists of a deity "Adivaraha Perumal", which is one of the 108 Vaishnaivaite deities.

Legends also tell us that King Dasaratha performed "Putra Kameshi Yagam" in the temple for the Birth of a child to his kingdom. The King performed pooja to the "Nabisthanam" of the goddess in the temple. King Dasaratha within a few months got a child. He belongs to the "Ekshuvagu Vamsam" where by the prime deity is Goddess Kamakshi. The extract of this story is visible in "Markendeya Puranam". The faith is, if prayed truly, the goddess provides children to childless couples.

2. ARULMIGU RAMANATHA SWAMY TEMPLE, RAMESWARAM

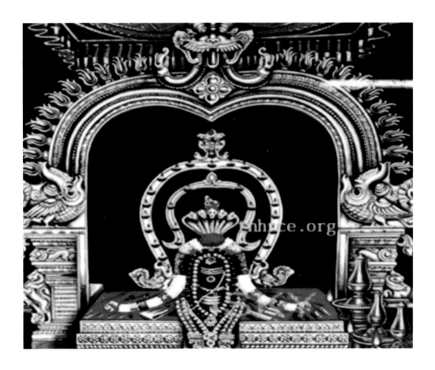

The temple and the island of Rameswaram have acquired this name because according to a legend, Lord Rama worshipped Lord Shiva, the God of Gods, here on return from Sri Lanka. According to the legend, after killing Ravana, Lord Rama returned with his consort Goddess Seetha to India first stepping on the shores of Rameswaram. To expiate the "dosha" of killing a Brahmin, Lord Rama wanted to offer worship to Lord

Shiva. Since there was no shrine in the island had despatched Sri Hanuman to Kailash to bring an idol of Lord Shiva.

The magnificent Ramanathaswamy temple is among the 12 Jyotirlingas in India. Jyotirlingam means the radiant sign of the almighty Shiva. It is believed that Lord Shiva first manisfested himself as a Jyotirlinga on the night of the Arudra Nakshatra. To the ordinary eye, there is nothing to distinguish the appearance, but it is believed that a person can see these Lingas as columns of fire piercing through the earth after he reaches a higher level of spiritual attainment.

This great Ramanathaswamy temple stands on a rising ground in the northern part of the island. This is one of the great fourteen sacred temples of the Pandyas. The temple was originally a thatched shed in charge of a hermit. The present structure of the temple is the result of the work of a number of personalities, who lived in different periods. According to the inscriptions available in the temple, it is believed that the ancient shrine at Rameshwaram was enlarged by King Parakramabahu of Sri Lanka in the 12th century A.D. and additions were made by the Pandyas, the Nayak rulers of Madurai and the Kings of Ramnad known as Sethupathis. Sethupathis or Sethukavalan were the custodians of the legendary bridge built by Lord Rama when he crossed the sea to reach Lanka (now Sri Lanka). Most of the later additions to this temple are ascribed to Sethupathis of Ramnad.

The temple buildings are surrounded by a high wall covering an area of about 865 feet from east to west and 657 feet from north to south. The gateway on the west is 78 feet high and is elaborately carved with mythological figures, its form being trapezoidal. The architecture resembles Egyptian style. The corridor of the Rameshwaram temple is known for its exquisite nature and probably in no other temples of India this particular feature can be found in such unparalleled magnificence. This beautiful structure enhances the devotion in the minds of the devotees as the serenity of that place is a captivating one. The neatness of the temple is also a notable feature. Among the Shiva temples, the temple at Rameshwaram is a more outstanding one due to various reasons such as sanctity and architecture.

A special feature in this temple is the large number of portrait sculptures. They are all of the Madurai Nayak Kings, such as Visvanatha Nayak, Krishnama Nayak, etc. Anuppu Mandapam, which has sculptures depicting scenes from Ramayana besides the statues of the Sethupathis, is an amusing one like those depicting a woman carrying a man on her shoulders and a man carrying a woman on his shoulders. Its interpretation is that while man generally should take care and provide for a woman, the positions will be reversed in the Kaliyuga. One noteworthy feature about the sculptures in this temple is the comparative dwarfish statue of the figures of the gatekeepers deposited over elephants in many places. In South Indian sculptural styles generally, there is a tendency to exaggerate certain features, like bosoms of female figures but at the same time, one must give credit to the sculptures for avoiding absolute nudity by the trailing of ornamental wreaths or garlands, where the design did not include a robe.

The Rameshwaram temple is probably the main reason for the town being known to every other person following Hinduism. Rameshwaram is believed to be the place from where Lord Rama started his journey to get his wife Sita back from Ravana and the Lord was helped by 'Vaanar-Sena', the army of legendary monkey-humans, and served by Hanuman, Lord Rama's paramount devotee. Also, many later versions of Ramayana testify of installing a Shiva Lingam by Shri Ram and Devi Sita to worship Lord Shiva as a part of penance for

Brahmahatya - killing of Brahmana, Ravana who was himself a well-known staunch follower of Lord Shiva. The Rameshwaram temple is believed to have the same Shiva Lingam.

The history of Rameswaram is centred on the island being a transit point to reach Sri Lanka (Ceylon historically) and the presence of Ramanathaswamy Temple. Tevaram, the 7th–8th century Tamil compositions on Shiva by the three prominent Nayanars (Saivites) namely Appar, Sundarar and Thirugnanasambandar offers rich tributes to this temple. The Chola king Rajendra Chola (1012–1040 CE) had a control of the town for a short period. The Jaffna kingdom (1215–1624 CE) had close connections with the island and claimed the title Setukavalan meaning custodians of the Rameswaram. Hinduism was their state religion and they made generous contribution to the temple. Setu was used in their coins as well as in inscriptions as marker of the dynasty.

According to Firishta, Malik Kafur, the head general of Alauddin Khilji, the ruler of Delhi Sultanate, reached Rameswaram during his political campaign in spite of stiff resistance from the Pandyan princes in the early 14th century. He erected a mosque by name Alia al-Din Khalji in honour of victory of Islam. During the early 15th century, the present day Ramanathapuram, Kamuthi and Rameswaram were included in the realms of the Pandya dynasty. In 1520 CE, the town came under the rule of Vijayanagara Empire. The Sethupathis, the breakaway from Madurai Nayaks, ruled Ramanathapuram and contributed to the Ramanathaswamy temple. The most notable of them are the contributions of Muthu Kumara Ragunatha and Muthu Ramalinga Sethupathi, who transformed the temple to an architectural ensemble. The region then fell under the rule of different rulers like Chanda Sahib (1740–1754 CE), Arcot Nawab and Muhammed Yusuf Khan (1725–1764 CE) in the middle of the 18th century. In 1795 CE, Rameswaram came under the direct control of the British East India Company and was annexed to the Madras Presidency. After 1947, the town became a part of Independent India.

According to mythology, Lord Rama (the seventh incarnation of Vishnu) built a bridge from Rameshwaram to Sri Lanka to rescue his wife Sita from the evil clutches of demon king Ravana. Hindus believe that visiting all the *Char Dham* will help them achieve *moksha* (liberation from rebirth).

Sri RamanathaswamyThirukoil

East and West Temple Towers

Ramanathaswamy Temple Corridor

Famous Temples in Tamil Nadu

3. ARUNACHALESVARA TEMPLE, THIRUVANNAMALAI

Thiruvannamalai is one of the most venerated places in Tamil Nadu. In ancient times, the term "Annamalai" meant an inaccessible mountain. The word "Thiru" was prefixed to signify its greatness, and coupled with the two terms, it is called Thiruvannamalai. Thiruvannamalai is one of the 'Panchbhuta sthalas' dedicated to Lord Shiva who appeared as a 'Jothi' or Fire and is being worshipped as a Jothi lingam. The name Thiruvannamalai is taken from the hill near the temple and the deity is called 'Arunachaleswarar'.

Thiruvannamalai is an important Shaivite centre of Tamil Nadu, famous for its impressive and historic temple of Arunachaleswara. During the Karthigai festival the entire Annamalai hill is lit up with thousands of lights. The hill is appropriately called in Sanskrit as Arunachala – or the Hill of Fire. The lord is worshipped here as the very incarnation of Fire, an element of Nature. The vast temple complex at the foot of the hill is one of the largest of its kind in Tamil Nadu and contains a number of inscriptions throwing valuable light on the history of the place. The temple has received the ode of the Tevaram hymns and also saint Manickavasagar. The presiding deity is described as a great effulgent fire, the dispeller of darkness and the symbol of purity. Later saints like Sekkilar and Arunagiri have also sung about the sacredness of the temple.

Arunachaleswarar Temple is an imposing structure, spread over more than 25 acres, with a marvellous architecture. It boasts four gateway towers known as gopurams, each of which is encompassed with mandapams, shrines and enclosures, decorated with finely carved sculptures and pillars. The eastern tower with 11 storeys, stands at a height of 66 m and is one of the largest temple towers in India. Also known as the Annamalaiyar Temple, it is dedicated to Lord Shiva and visited by devotees in large numbers from all parts of the country. Built in the traditional Dravidian style of architecture, the temple is believed to be the eighth-largest Hindu temple in the world.

The temple complex houses many halls and the most popular one is the thousand-pillared hall, which was constructed during the Vijayanagar period (1336-1646). The temple is one of the panchabhootasthalams, which are dedicated to the manifestation of Lord Shiva as five natural elements. Legend has it that the lord has apparently manifested himself as the element fire in this temple.

Arunachaleswarar temple houses eight lingams known as ashtalingam, which are positioned at different locations facing different directions. These lingams are named as Indralingam, Agnilingam, Yamalingam, Niruthilingam, Varunalingam, Vayulingam, Kuberalingam and Esanyalingam. Each lingam signifies different directions of the earth and is believed to bless the devotees who undertake Girivalam, a popular religious ritual, with different benefits. The temple remains open from 5.30 am to 9 pm every day.

The walls on the east and west measure 700 ft (210 m), the ones on the south 1,479 ft (451 m), and those on the north 1,590 ft (480 m). The present masonry and towers date back to the 9th century CE, as seen from an inscription in the structure made by Chola kings who ruled at that time. Other inscriptions hint of its antiquity dating even before the 9th century.

It has four gateway towers, the gopuram, on its four sides. The eastern tower, the Rajagopuram, is the tallest in the temple. The base of the Rajagopuram is made of granite, measuring 135 ft (41 m) by 98 ft (30 m). It was begun by king Krishnadevaraya (1509–29 CE) of the Vijayanagara dynasty, and completed by Sevappa Nayaka (1532–80 CE). The inscriptions indicate that the tower was built at the behest of Sivanesa and his brother Lokanatha in 1572 CE.

The south tower is called Thirumanjangopuram, and the west, Pei Gopuram. Raghunathabhyudayam and Sangitha Sudha, both Nayak era scriptures, also describe the towers. The 'Tanjavuri Andhra Raja Charitamu' mentions that Krishnadevaraya built the main tower and the outer precincts of the temple. The temple has a total of five precincts, each of which holds a huge Nandi, the sacred bull of Shiva. Towers include the Vallala Maharaja Gopuram and Kili Gopuram, or Parrot Tower.

The temple celebrates dozens of festivals throughout the year. Four prime festivals, the Brahmotsavam, are celebrated yearly. The most important of these lasts ten days during the Tamil month of Karthikai, between November and December, concluding with the celebration of Karthikai Deepam. A huge lamp is lit in a cauldron, at the top of the Arunachala hills during the Deepam. To mark the occasion, the festival image of Arunachalesvara is taken on the wooden chariot around the mountain. Inscriptions indicate that the festival was celebrated as early as from during the Chola period (from 850 CE to 1280 CE).

Every full moon, millions of pilgrims offer their prayers to Lord Arunachalesvara by circumambulating the hill barefoot. The circumambulation covers a distance of 14 kilometres (8.7 miles), and is referred as Girivalam. According to Hindu legend, the walk removes sins, fulfils desires and helps achieve freedom from the cycle of birth and rebirth. Offerings are made in a string of tanks, shrines, pillared meditation halls, springs and caves around the hill. The circumambulation continues during the rest of the month. On the day of yearly Chitra Pournami, the full moon of the Tamil calendar, hundreds of thousands of pilgrims come from across the world to worship Arunachalesvara. It is learnt that Saint Arunagirinathar lived and wrote hymns in Tiruvannamalai in the fourteenth century. It also learnt that Sri Ramana Maharishi lived in Tiruvannamalai.

Karthigai is the name of both a month and nakshatra in the Tamil calendar. The month corresponds to November-December and the nakshatra is plaiding according to the legends have grown around this karthigai festival. The constellation Karthigai appears as a group of six seats in the firmament, in the shape of a pendant from the ear. The stars are considered in Indian mythology as the six celestial nymphs who reared the six-faced Muruga in infancy in the Saravana tank. Muruga is consequently called Karthikeya, one brought up by the Karthika nymphs. Usually the annual Karthigai festival is celebrated in Tamil Nadu when the moon is in conjunction with the asterism Karthigai. This is especially important in Thiruvannamalai for various reasons. In memory of this Light, the whole temple is illuminated with thousands of lamps, big and small, and every home is also illuminated in the evening with hundreds of lamps. It is indeed a grand sight to see the temple tower lights shedding their twinkling light throughout the darkness of the whole night. A special offering is made to Shiva on this day, consisting of fried or puffed rice mixed with treacle. In the city of Thiruvannamalai, the same procedure is adopted for the festival even today. Hundreds of thousands of devotees and pilgrims gather in the outer courtyards for the temple from early afternoon waiting for the appropriate time in the evening when the symbolic fire will be lit. Sri Arunachaleswara is taken in a procession around the courtyard. At the appointed time (usually about 5 p.m) the fire on the hill in the background is lit. This fire is made of vast quantities of camphor supported by more than a hundred liters of ghee. The fire continues to burn for the whole of the night and is visible even at a distance of eight miles. It continues for several days and nights following the moment the fire is lit on the hill; a deepa – aradhana (waving of camphor lamp) is made to Sri Arunachaleswara. The assembled bhaktas have a simultaneous darsan of the Lord in the temple as also of the column of Light on the hill.

Five temple cars, called Ther in Tamil, with wooden carvings, are used for the procession. Tiruvoodal is another festival celebrated during the first week of the Tamil month Thai at mid-January of every year. On the morning of Maatu Pongal, between 15th and 16th January, Nandi is decorated with garlands made of fruits, vegetables and sweets. The festival deities of Arunachalesvara and Unnamamulai Amman are taken out of the temple to Tiruoodal street to enact the oodal (or love tiff) between the two in the evening. The Hill (Linga) removes the sin from all the worlds, and sins bondage (Runa) becomes non-existent when one sees it.

Full View of Tiruvannamali Temple

Chitra Pournami (a festival) - Tiruvannamalai Temple

Famous Temples in Tamil Nadu

Kaartikai Deepam

4. THIRUCHENDUR MURUGAN TEMPLE

The Thiruchendur Murugan temple is an ancient Hindu temple dedicated to lord Murugan situated in Tamil Nadu, India. The puranic name or historical name for this temple is Jayanthipuram. It is located in the eastern end of the town Thiruchendur in the district of Tuticorin. It is 60 km south-east of Tirunelveli, 40 km from Tuticorin and 75 km north-east of Kanyakumari. The temple complex is on the shores of the Bay of Bengal.

Thiruchendur is one of the six holy centers celebrated for the worship of Lord Murugan. While the remaining five spots are on top of a hill, this is the only place that is on the seashore in a picturesque setting. There is a traditional version about this place that Lord Murugan had his army stationed here before finally destroying the arms of Surapadma, whose fort was located in the widest of ocean called Viramahendrapuram. Festivals commemorating the lord's conquest of Surapadma are being celebrated annually. There is mention about this temple in the Tamil classics of the Sangam era. Purananuru eulogises this place. This place has been praised in Thirumurukaruppadai. Saint Arunagirinather in his Tiruppugal has devoted eighty six songs in praise of this place.

No record exists on the year of actual construction of the temple, but there are records of improvements to the temple by Pandya and Chera Kingdoms. However, early Sangam poetry refers to the Murugan seashore shrine at Tirrucciralaivay, which is thought to refer to the Thiruchendur Temple. The earliest existing inscription at the temple is dated 875 AD, and talks about a Pandyan called Varekuna Maran.

The Pandya and the Chera, their vassals, and other men of devotion further improved the temple. Maharaja Marthandavarma (1729-58 AD), the maker of modern Travancore, endowed the very first -- the Udaya-Marthanda Kattalai of each morning -- more than two centuries ago; and others followed in the nine arathanas of the day. As time rolled on, the effect of the sea and its salt-laden air began to tell upon the inferior sandstones used at the first instance in the original construction.

The temple was fully constructed anew in all its details, and Kumbhabhishekam performed in 1941. The temple and its gopuram of nine floors, built on the extremity of the sandstone cliff are a landmark, and visible from sea for twelve miles around, looking as has been said like a ship in full sail. There is an interesting departure from the standard temple architectural practice in the case of the Thiruchendur Murugan temple; the Rajagopuram of this temple is in the west, whereas Rajagopurams, as a rule form the main entrance to a temple in the east. The reason probably was the fear of damage to the Rajagopuram, due to proximity of the seashore to the temple in the east.

Thiruchendur means sacred and beautiful town in Tamil. The temple is dedicated to Murugan, the warrior deity and second son of Shiva. When Murugan came here for the conquest along with his army, he found it to be very small and ordered the celestial architect Viswakarma to expand it.

Lord Murugan won and accepted Soorapadman on Sashti (sixth day) of the waxing moon (bright) night (Valar Pirai) of the month Aippasi. This day is celebrated as 'Kanda Sashti'. This incident happened at Thiruchendur and hence, the 'Kanda Sashti' festival is celebrated in this place with all grandeur.

In devotional literature and in the Tirumurugarruppadai, the earliest account of his worship, six chosen spots in the Tamil land are referred to by Nakkirar as of more than ordinary sanctity for his worship, and thereby favoured by him. Tiruchendur occupies among them the second place in his order.

The temple celebrates Lord Murugan's divine mission to free the Devas, and the vanquishment of Surapatuma and his mighty hosts in "Vîra-mahendram", their mid-ocean fortress nearby. As such, the puranas narrate that the Devas gained their deliverance from the Asuras like Anamughan, Panumughan, Simhamughan, and Soorapadman by his grace.

The temple is a fitting abode for an immensely powerful deity. The Thiruchendur Murugan temple is believed to be one of the six abodes of Lord Murugan. It is a temple that has been in existence for millennia, according to ancient Hindu scripts.

யாமிருக்க   பயமேன்!

Thiruchendur Murugan

Dutch Tried to Steal Thiruchendur Murugan

Famous Temples in Tamil Nadu   29

Front View of Temple

5. ARULMIGU SRI PARTHASARATHY SWAMY TEMPLE, THIRUVALLIKENI

The Parthasarathy Swamy temple, one of the 108 Divya Desams, is said to have been renovated by a King of Pallava dynasty. "Brindaranya" is the traditional Puranic name of Thiru-Alli-Keni now known as Thiruvallikeni or modern

Triplicane. It is said that for at least five thousand years, it has been a resting place for pilgrims who had come down from Thirupathy to have a bath in the sea on the days of Solar and Lunar Eclipses and on other auspicious days, it being in a direct line to Thirupathy, Thiruthani and Trivellore and the route being free from swamps. According to Brahmanda Puranam, the five Deities in the temple are said to have been worshipped by the Saptah Rishis viz. Bhrigu, Manchi, Atri, Markandeya, Sumathi, Saptharoma and Jabali and also have been praised by two of the earliest Azhwars viz. Thirumazhisai Azhwar, Peyazhwar and later on by Thirumangaimannan or Kaliyan, who is considered to be the last of the Alzhars.

The presiding Deity of this temple, Sri Venkatakrishna Swami is also known as "GEETHACHARYA". According to Brahmandapurana, a king named Sumathy prayed Lord Thiruvengada of the Seven Hills to give him darshan in the form of the Charioteer (SARATHY) to PARTHA during the MAHABHARATHA WAR and rendering GEETHA. Lord Thiruvengada appeared in his dream and bade him to go to "BRINDARANYA" where he would give him Darshan in the form he wished.

The central figure enshrined in the sanctum sanctorum is being worshipped as "SRI VENKATAKRISHNA SWAMY". Sri Rukmani Thayar and Satyaki, his younger brother, are installed on his right and left side respectively. His elder brother Balarama is seen on the right side of Rukmani Thayar facing north and his son Prathyumnan and his grandson Anirudhan are seen on the northern side of the Garbagraha facing south. These five warriors (Pancha Veerar) are so placed in these positions as we now worship them to keep in conformity with some incidents that took place in their life-time. Still more grandeur and inspiring is the bewitching and ever smiling UTHSAVAR Deity – Sri Parthasarathy Swami, with marks in the face caused by Bhishma's arrows during the Mahabharatha War. As per Mahabharatha, Vishnu, in his avatar as Krishna was acting as charioteer for Arjuna, the Pandava prince during the war with Kauravas. Krishna did not take any weapons during the war. During the fight between Arjuna and Bhishma, Krishna was injured by the arrow from Bhishma. The mark in the image in the temple is believed to follow the legend. The Thilagam set with diamonds with a Saffire in the centre resembles the full moon in the crystal clear blue sky.

The place is called Allikeni, meaning a pond of lily as it is believed that historically the place was full of lily ponds. The place is the only place where the presiding deity is sported with a mustache. As per another legend, the place was once a Tulsi forest. A king named Sumati wanted to see Vishnu in the form of Parthasarathi and prayed at Srinivasa temple in Tirupathi. Srinivasa directed the king to visit the temple here built by sage Atreya and worshipped with another sage called Sumati.

Famous Temples in Tamil Nadu

6. KAPALEESWARAR TEMPLE, CHENNAI

Shri Kapaleeswarar temple is a majestic piece of exciting architecture located in the city of Chennai. It is situated in Mylapore and was built during the reign of the Pallavas in 7th Century CE. The name Mylapore is derived from the legend that the Goddess Uma worshipped Shiva in the form of a peacock (mayil in Tamil). We can see a representation of this legend on stone in a small Shrine under a Punnai tree (Sthala Vriksha) in the Courtyard of the temple. Claudius Ptolemy, the Greek Geographer (AD 85 - AD 165) has referred to Mylapore in his books as 'Millarpha'. It was apparently a well-known sea port town with a flourishing trade. It must have also been a place of culture, as Saint, Tiruvalluvar the celebrated author of Tirukkural, the famous ethical treatise, is believed to have lived in Mylapore nearly 2,000 years ago.

St. Thomas, one of the apostles of Jesus, is reported to have visited Mylapore in the 2nd Century A.D. His tomb is in the St. Thomas basilica, a beautiful Cathedral about half a mile from the temple.

The presiding deity of Shri Kapaleeshwar resides in the magnificent temple which is one of the 276 Thevara Paadal Petra Shiva Sthalam. The Saivite Saints of the 7th Century, Saint Sambandar and Saint Appar, have sung about the Shrine in their hymns. It is the 24th Shiva temple in the Thondai Nadu-Nadunadu region praised in the Thevaram hymns. It is convincingly believed by the masses of the local community that the almighty Lord Shiva is self-manifested in this fantastic Temple. Interestingly, it is a very important place, being the most popular Sapthasthana temple in Chennai. The Kapaleeswarar temple is also known to be the birthplace of Vayilar Nayanar, one of the 63 Nayanmars.

The beauty of the grand temple can be witnessed with the 70 ft main building which also includes two corridors surrounding the east. It is a very important fact that this is a newly built temple because of the original temple being submerged into the sea. Presently visited temple is approximately three hundred and fifty years old.

Though the clear picture about who built the temple is not known, it is commonly believed that the temple was originally built by Pallavas in the seventh century CE due to its reference in the hymns of the Nayanmars; however, the architecture of the temple seems to be just 300-400 years old. The scholars have concluded that the original temple was built at the seashore in 7th century by Pallavas and was destroyed by Portuguese. The temple existing today about 1 km far from the shore was built by Vijay Nagar kings during 16th century.

There are inscriptions dating back to 12th century inside the temple. The temple's 120 ft gopuram (gateway tower) was built during 1906 with stucco figures adorning it. The temple is maintained and administered by the Hindu Religious and Endowment Board of the Government of Tamil Nadu.

There are many tales that proves the significance of this Kapaleeswarar Temple. Lord Murugan, son of Lord Shiva visited this temple and worshipped him and his mother Goddess Uma (Karpagambal) before heading to a war with an Asura (demon) named Surapadman. He received the Shaktivel here at this temple, a divine powerful weapon his mother gave to fight the Asura.

Now there is another fascinating legend of why Lord Shiva is known as Kapaleeshwarar. Once Lord Brahma, the creator as per Hindu mythology, considering himself greater than Lord Shiva as he had five heads, failed to show proper respects to Lord Shiva. The Lord Shiva, in order to teach Brahma a lesson in humility, nipped one of the five heads of Brahma and held his skull in his hand, earning himself the name Kapaleeswarar for Kapalam in Sanskrit means Skull.

Thai Poosam is an important month celebrated in this temple. It is believed to be the day, when Lord Shiva with Mother Uma granted His dancing darshan to Lord Vishnu, Lord Brahma,

Sages Vyakrapada and Patanjali and the 3000 Brahmins of Thillai Chidambaram. It is believed that worshipping Lord Shiva this day, takes the devotee to an eternal bliss.

7. KAILASANATHAR TEMPLE

The Kanchi Kailasanathar temple is the oldest structure in Kanchipuram. It is a Hindu temple in the Tamil architectural style. It is dedicated to Lord Shiva, and is known for its historical importance. The temples at Kanchipuram reveal the level of Architectural elegance attained during the early period of history. Among them, the most architecturally elegant temple is the Kailasanathar temple. The temple was built between 685-705 AD by Rajasimha (Narasimhavarman II), ruler of the Pallava Dynasty. His other structural temples are shore temple at Mahabalipuram and Talagriveswara temple at Panamalai etc.

The plan of this temple is comprised of a large and a smaller courtyard with central group of shrines placed towards the western extremity of the large ones. The shrine is surmounted by lofty pyramidal tower. The low-slung sandstone compound contains a large number of carvings, including many half-animal deities, which were popular during the early Pallava architectural period. The structure contains 58 small shrines which are dedicated to various forms of Lord Shiva. These are built into niches on the inner face of the high compound wall of the circumambulatory passage. The sanctum consists of a panel of Somaskanda, the depiction of Shiva, Parvathi and Skanda in the centre, carved at the back wall, which is a characteristic feature of all temples built during Raja Simha's period. The wall of this temple is surfaced with sculptures. The shrines are topped by shikaras. The sanctum is crowned by an octagonal shikhara and a stupi. The temple is one of the most prominent tourist attractions of the city.

It is the first structural temple built in South India by Narasimhavarman II (Rajasimha), and who is also known as Rajasimha Pallaveswaram. His son, Mahendravarman III, completed the front façade and the gopuram (tower). Earlier temples were either built of wood or hewn into rock faces in caves or on boulders, as seen in Mahabalipuram. The Kailasanathar temple became the trendsetter for other similar temples in South India. The Vimana of the Kailasanathar temple is an example of progressive multiplication. A transformation from unity to multiplicity is expressed by an expanding, proliferating pattern. A single element begins a sequence of rows in which the number of elements progressively increases. In the South Indian temple architecture (Dravidian style), the super structure of the Vimana or its several storeys are set with small temple shapes, similar to the original shape. The smaller shapes are aligned in a definite pattern at each horizontal level, the repetition of these shapes at each band forming a kind of garland at each level. The repetition of identical shapes either in the vertical or in the horizontal, or vertically as well as horizontally, is another frequently used procedure to add visual complexity to the temple form. According to local belief, the temple was a safe sanctuary for the rulers of the kingdom during wars. A secret tunnel, built by the kings, was used as an escape route and is still visible. It is believed that Raja Raj Chola I (985–1014 CE) visited the temple and drew inspiration from this temple to build the Brihadeeswara Temple. Currently, Kanchi Kailasanathar temple is maintained by the Archaeological Survey of India (ASI).

The temple is located on the banks of the Vegavathy river at the western limits of the Kanchipuram. It faces east. Its location, demarcated according to the religious faiths, is in one of three "Kanchis", the Shiva Kanchi; the other two Kanchis are, Vishnu Kanchi and Jain Kanchi. It is 75 kilometres (47 miles) from Chennai, the capital city of Tamil Nadu. Kailasanathar is one of several notable temples in Kanchipuram, the others being Ekambaranatha, Kachapeshwarar, Kamakshi Amman, Kumarakottam temple, and Varadaraja Perumal. The Kailasanathar temple (meaning: "Lord of the Cosmic Mountain"), is built in the tradition of Smartha worship of Shiva, Vishnu, Devi, Surya (Sun), Ganesha and Kartikeya, in Hinduism, a practice which replaced Buddhism.

Temple construction is credited to the Pallava dynasty, who had established their kingdom with Kanchipuram (also known as "Kanchi" or "Shiva Vishnu Kanchi") as the capital city, considered one of the seven sacred cities under Hinduism. In Kanchi, after the Pallavas expanded their territories to the north, west and south both within Tamil, Andhra and Kannada territories under Emperor Narasimhavarman I, they started expanding their capital city of Kanchipuram and built many temples of great magnificence. Among the two unique specimens of temple architecture of the period 640-730 AD are the Thiru Parameswara Vinnagaram, which is also known as the Vaikunta Perumal temple and the Kailasanathar temple.

The temple has retained the Pallava architecture in its original stylized form with influence of the later styles developed by the Chola Dynasty and Vijayanagara Emperors. It is of stone built architecture unlike the rock cut architecture built into hallowed caves or carved into rock outcrops as in Mahabalipuram. The tall gopuram (tower) is to the left and the temple complex is to the right. The temple's foundations are made of granite, which could withstand the weight of the temple, while the superstructure, including the carvings, is all made of sandstone. Initially, only the main sanctuary existed with pyramidal vimana and a detached mandapa (main hall).

Maha Shivaratri is the biggest festival held in the temple when thousand of devotees throng the temple in the evening hours to offer prayers to the main deity.

8. NAGARAJA TEMPLE, NAGERCOIL

Nagaraja temple is a Hindu temple worshipping Nagaraja (The King of Serpents- Vasuki) situated at the heart of Nagercoil town. The name for the town Nagercoil originated from this temple. The temple has innumerable statues of serpents. It is built in the Chera architectural style. The temple has two main deities, Krishna (reverred as Ananda Krishna) and Nagaraja. The upadevathas are Shiva, Subrahmanya Swami, Ganesha, Devi and Dwarapalaka. In conformity with an ancient tradition the priests are Namboothiri Brahmins who are referred to as Pambumekkatmana in Thrissur, Kerala. The temple has a vast pond. Devotees offer milk and turmeric powder as a part of their prayers to the Nagas in the temple. The temple is open from 4.00 a.m. to 11.30 a.m. and from 5.00 p.m. to 8.30 p.m. It is difficult to ascertain the exact age of the temple.

The original name of this area is called Anantha - Samudram as per the records. It was once a popular Brahmin agrahara. It was originally a Jain temple. The temple is surrounded by paddy fields, flower gardens and coconut trees. The Nanthavanam (temple garden) is noted for its flower called 'Naga flower', a symbolic representation of Nagaraja. It is believed that there are plenty of cobras inside the temple premises which guard the temple. Though there are plenty of snakes, no fatal case of snakebite has ever occurred anywhere around the area.

It is believed that veneration of snakes began around 4000 B.C. In Ramayana, there are references about the mountain Mahendragiri which provided settlements to the Nagas. From this, it is assumed that the origin of Naga worship in the surrounding areas of Nagercoil goes back to very early times. The architecture of Nagaraja temple is based on the Kerala style. As the Nagaraja temple is Jain in origin, the images of Vardhamana Mahaveera, Parsvanath and Padmavathy are sculpted in the pillars of the Artha mandapa of the temple. The flag-staff facing the principal deity in the outer prakara of the temple is considered as the 'Karuna Linga'.

The sanctum is a simple thatched shed, with mud walls. It enshrines the King of Serpents. It is believed that snakebite is not fatal within a kilometer distance of the temple. The fane has some Jain sculptures. So it is believed that it was a Jain school anciently. This temple had four ponds; out of which two were filled and renamed as Nagarajathidal (south) and Anna stadium (north). Another one is not used by devotees because of its polluted condition. The tank inside the temple area is now known as temple tank for Nagaraja temple. The tank is in rectangular shape. Its size is 82 × 56 × 12 ft. The temple tank water is used by devotees for bathing and for the various rituals in the temple.

There is no authentic epigraph to aid the historian with its chronology. The mountain Mahendragiri in the Kanyakumari district is referred to as the abode of Nagas in the Ramayana of Valmiki. From this, it can be presumed that the origin of Naga influence in the area goes back to legendary times. The story behind the existence of this temple is as follows - once a Namboothiri, a great devotee of Lord Shiva did Bhajanam [worship] for twelve days at Thiruvanchikkulam temple. A pleased Lord Shiva asked Vasuki, the Nagaraja to grant Darshan [sight of] to the Namboothiri. Vasuki did as his lord asked, visited the Namboothiri and gifted him the Nagamanickam to eliminate his sufferings. From that day, the Namboothiri worshipped Nagaraja and Nagayakshi [Queen of the Nagas]. One day, returning back after curing a Pandya King's skin disease, he reached Kottar, which is now known as Nagercoil. Suddenly he heard a woman crying. When he reached where the woman was standing he was surprised to see blood coming out of a rock. Immediately he identified it as the idol of the five headed Nagaraja. He did all the necessary rituals and built a small temple around it. Since then the Nagaraja is worshipped there. The present day temple was constructed later with shrines of Maha Vishnu and Shiva. On the pillars of the temple, there are many images of Jain monks known as Thirthankaras. At the time of reconstruction and renovation in the year 1535 the temple might have passed in to the hands of the Hindus. This temple is a fine example of the transformation of a Jain temple into a Hindu shrine.

The most auspicious occasion of the Nagaraja Temple is the Ayilyam festival during the Malayalam month Thula

[October-November]. A12-day pooja is conducted which include a special Tantric rituals. The Brahmotsavam during the January-February month is also a major festive occasion at Nagaraja Temple, Nagercoil. Navarathri festival celebrated during the months of September-October and Thirukarthigai in November-December are other festivals celebrated in the temple.

The temple of Nagaraja at Nagercoil unifies the four streams of Indian religion Saivism, Vaishnavism, Jainism and Buddhism is a fine example of religious integration. The temple also serves as an arena of sports. On Shivarathiri several devotees start from the temple at Thirumalai and finish their marathon pilgrimage at Nattalam covering nearly 100 km. in 12 hours. That is called as Shivalayaottam. Thus, we have seen the Hindu temples were not only the places of worship but the very focus of society.

The Nagaraja temple has many idols of the serpent Gods, the main deities are Lord Krishna and Lord Nagaraja. Devotees offer milk and turmeric to the serpent God. This temple gives a unique prasad "Mannu" (Sand) to the devotees. This temple is popular for the ritual Naga Sarpa Dosh. The temple is vast and has a beautiful pond. Devotees get the holy dip in the water and seek the blessings of the serpent God.

Famous Temples in Tamil Nadu

9. SARVANI SHAKTIPEETH SHRI BHAGAVATHY TEMPLE

The temple is dedicated to the patron deity of Kanyakumari, Devi Kumari. The temple is said to have been built around 3000 years ago by Parashurama, and is also one of the Shakthi Peethas that are spread across various locations in the country. One day Banasura tried to woo the Devi to marry him. The goddess denied and got into a fierce battle with him, demolishing the demon king at Kanyakumari, as a punishment for his wrong deeds. Sage Parasurama built a shrine to Devi Kanyakumari and installed her beautiful idol in the temple.

Devi Kanyakumari is goddess Parvati in the form of an adolescent girl child. Devi is also known as Shree Baala Bhadra or Shree Baala. She is popularly known as "sakthi" (Durga or Parvati) "Devi". The Bhagavathy temple is located in Cape Kanyakumari in Tamil Nadu, at the southern tip of main land India, there by located on the confluence of the Bay of Bengal, the Arabian Sea, and the Indian Ocean. She is also known by several other names, including Kanya Devi and Devi Kumari. She is also worshiped as Shree Bhadrakali by devotees. Devi Kanyakumari has been mentioned in the Ramayana, the Mahabharata, and the Sangam works of Manimekalai, Puranaanooru and Narayana Upanishad. Sage Parashurama is said to have performed the consecration of the temple. As directed by his Guru, Sri Ramakrishna Paramahamsa, Swami Vivekananda came here to seek the Devi's blessing in December 1892. It is in this location that he decided to embark on missionary work through a higher level of action, rather than being passive like the usual sanyasis. The goddess is believed to be the one who removes rigidity of the mind; devotees usually feel the tears in their eyes or even inside their mind when they pray to the goddess in devotion and contemplation.

Kanyakumari Temple is one of the 52 Shakti Peethams. It is believed that the right shoulder and (back) spine area of Sati's corpse fell here creating the presence of Kundalinisakthi in the region. Devi Kanyakumari has been mentioned in Ramayana, Mahabharata, and the Sangam works of Manimekalai,

Puranaanooru and Nārāyana (Mahānārāyana) Upanishad, a Vaishnava upanishad in the Taittiriya Samhita of Krishna Yajur Veda.

The mythological story dates back to the prehistoric Tamil period. Bana, an asura by birth was the ruler of his land. He was a very powerful king. He practiced tapasya and obtained a boon from Lord Brahma that his death will only be by an adolescent young girl. With this powerful boon, he became fearless and wreaked havoc on the entire world. It was the Devi who took the form of a girl and vanquished the demon.

The presiding image is sported in standing posture with an Akshamala in her hands. There is an image of a lion in her pedestal indicating that she is the form of Durga. There is a four-pillared hall in the temple, each of which gives out sounds of Veena (a string instrument), Mrudanga (a percussion instrument), flute and Jalatharanga (porcelain instrument). Devi Kanyakumari is the goddess of virginity and penance. It was a practice that people chose to receive the Diksha of Sanyasa from here in older times. The rites and rituals of the temple are organized and classified according to Sankaracharya's treatise.

Red Sarees and Ghee wick lamps are offered to the goddess by devotees. Reciting Lalita-Sahasranama while approaching and circumambulating the temple is considered auspicious. The location of Kanyakumari, i.e. the southern tip of India has been held sacred by Hindus' as it is the confluence of three seas. Offering Pitru Tarpan and bathing in the sea in the Kanyakumari beach is considered holy because it is the convergence of many important Theertham. There are a total of 11 Theerthams associated with the temple in the ocean surrounding Kanyakumari.

Famous Temples in Tamil Nadu

10. SRI LAKSHMI NARAYANI GOLDEN TEMPLE

The Golden Temple of Vellore is situated in a place called "Malaikodi". The temple held its consecration on the 24th of August in the year 2007. This ceremony was attended by thousands of devotees. Thus, the Golden Temple history does not date back to the era of Vijayanagara kings when the majority of the construction in the city was done. The god form in the Lakshminarayani temple is Goddess Mahalakshmi. As per Hindu mythology, the name 'Lakshmi' is synonymous with wealth and abundance, mainly gold jewellery and gold coins. An image of a beautiful goddess draped in a red sari, bejewelled with gold ornaments and showering gold coins. This is Goddess

Lakshmi, regarded as the Goddess of wealth, fortune and beauty. Goddess Lakshmi's marriage with Lord Vishnu is the paradigm for traditional Hindu weddings.

Lakshmi is sometimes shown with one or two elephants and occasionally with an owl. Elephants symbolise work, activity and strength, as well as water, rain and fertility for abundant prosperity. The owl signifies the patient striving to observe, see and discover knowledge particularly when surrounded by darkness. As a bird reputedly blinded by daylight, the owl also serves as a symbolic reminder to refrain from blindness and greed after knowledge and wealth has been acquired.

The temple has been worked on by highly adept artisans. They have done intricate and manual work to create this mammoth. The temple has been built on 100 acres of land. It has been designed by a Vellore-based architect, Sri Narayani Peedam. This has been advanced by Sri Sakthi Amma, also known Narayani Amma, who is a Vellore-based religious leader.

The forehead or crown of the Temple has some of the most intricate designs ever seen in the Indian construction. It is carved with complex art forms in gold and silver. The development of this awe-inspiring forehead was completed on 24th August 2007. It is believed that more than 1500 kg of gold was used to make the forehead.

The crown of Sri Lakshmi Golden Temple is called "Vimanam" or "Ardha Mandapam". This crown is one of the biggest temple crowns in the history of architecture. The temple is the storehouse of the diety of Sri Lakshmi Narayani. Sripuram Golden Temple was built in a time frame of 7 years. This period is considerably small when considering the construction of other massive buildings and temples like Taj Mahal was completed in 22 years, Golden Temple, Amritsar, Punjab, was completed in around 10 years etc. The temple with its gold covering, has intricate work done by artisans specialising in temple art using gold. Every single detail was manually created, including converting the gold bars into gold foils and then mounting the foils on copper. Gold foil from 9 layers to 10 layers has been mounted on the etched copper plates. Every single detail in the temple art has significance from the Vedas.

Sripuram's design features a star-shaped path (Sri Chakra), positioned in the middle of the lush green landscape, with a length of over 1.8 km. As one walks along this 'starpath' to reach the temple in the middle, one can also read various spiritual messages such as the gift of the human birth itself, and the value of spirituality along the way. Despite being religiously tolerant, the heads of the temple are not lenient on the outfit of the visitors. Like the dress code of any other temple, the Vellore Golden Temple dress code is also a strict one. A casual and elegant outfit is the best when visiting the temple. One should avoid any kind of extravagant outfit. When opting for any Western outfit, ensure that its length is well below your knees. Carrying any kind of head cover such as dupatta, scarf or handkerchief is the best practise. So, overall Sri Lakshmi Narayani Golden temple is the best temple to visit. Many devotees stated that they felt happier than ever after visiting the temple. They also felt some positive energy around them.

11. SIRUVAPURI MURUGAN TEMPLE

Siruvapuri is located about 40 kms from Chennai on the Chennai-Kolkata highway. The temple is located about 3 km off the highway. History of the temple has that Lava and Kusa, the sons of Rama lived in this place. Once when Rama was passing this place, the youngsters fought a battle with Rama himself without knowing that he was their father. As the young children waged a war here, the place was called as Siruvar Por Puri. (Siruvar means children, Por Puri means waging a war, in Thamizh). This place is now called as Chinnambedu, which originally was Siruvar Ambu Edu (children who took their arrows for the fight).

Some hundreds of years back there lived a lady called Murugammai in this village. She had been a very ardent devotee of Lord Murugan here. She always used to chant his name and pray him, for years. Her husband who didn't like her worshipping all the time was warning her to stop it. But she never listened to him. One day, her husband cut her arms off out of anger. Even then, Murugammai cried for help only with Lord Murugan. The Lord who was pleased with her bhakti, that he made her hands join even without the signs of any wound.

Lord Murugan here is called Śrī Balasubramanyar and is said to be powerful, granting the wishes of devotees. This beautiful temple also has Śrī Annamalaiyar (Lord Shiva) and Śrī Unnamulai Amman. The utsavamoorthy of Lord Muruga is seen as Valli-Manalar in a wedding posture with ŚrīValli. Lord Murugan here is believed to grant wishes for those intend to buy or construct a house. Many people who wish to buy a house visit Lord Muruga here for blessings to fulfill their wish.

Among the various names of Murukan, the name Valli-Kanavan (Valli's husband) stands supreme as the famous one. Murukan, who is the consort of Teyvayānai, the celestial daughter of Indra, married a huntress-girl of this human world, an aspect having very deep philosophical significance. All are equal in the face of God and this is the expression of the Vallināyakam form. Valli shines in brilliance here as Ichhā-Śakti. The marriage of Murukan with Valli is eulogised by Tamil scholars as a most fitting example of 'furtive love' (kalavumanam). Murukan married Valli and enjoyed conjugal bliss with her with a smile always. This is indicative of how the householders' life should be led in this mundane world. His image of wedlock with Valli is known as Valli Kalyāna-Sundarar. The Kumāra Tantra depicts this form as having one face and four hands. The front two hands are one in abhayamudrā and the other in Kadyavalmpītham (hand placed on the hip). In the back, in his two hands, he has rudraksamāla and kamandalu. In this form on the right side we find Valli in all her beauty.

A unique feature of this temple is the Maragatha Mayil (Peacock) the carrier of Lord Murugan made of green stone. Arunagirinathar is seen just near the sanctum facing the Lord. Arunagirinathar has visited this temple and sung many Thiruppugazh songs here. He also has composed an Archanai Thiruppugazh on Lord Muruga, which if recited fulfils ones wishes. Other deities are Maragatha Vinayakar, Aadhi Murugar, Naagar, Venkatrayar, Muniswaraar and Bairavar

Lord Murugan holding the hand of Valli in preparation for wedlock is only the one of its kind at Ciruvāpuri Śrī Bālasubramanya Svāmi Temple. The worship of Valli Kalyana Sundarar paves the way for the celebration of marriages at the proper time among families. Even marriages which have been thwarted by circumstances are said to get relieved of obstacles, paving the way for happy married life.

12. PALANI MURUGAN TEMPLE

Arulmigu Dandayudhapani Swami Temple is one of the Aaru-Padaiveedu (Six Abodes of Murugan). It is located in the city of Palani in Dindigul district, 150 kilometres (94 miles) southeast of Coimbatore and northwest of Madurai in the foothills of the Palani Hills, Tamil Nadu, India. Palani has been mentioned in the Sangam literature as 'Podhini'. In the 'Thirumurugaatruppadai', composed by the great Tamil poet, Nakkeerar, Palani has been mentioned as the third abode (Padai-veedu) of the Lord Murugan. The idol of the Murugan in Palani was created and consecrated by sage Bogar, one of Hinduism's eighteen great Siddha gurus, out of an amalgam of nine poisons or navapashanam. According to legends the 'Navapashanam' consists of 'Veeram', 'Pooram', 'Rasam', 'Jathilingam', 'Kandagam', 'Gauri Pashanam', 'Vellai Pashanam', 'Mridharsingh' and 'Silasat'. The legend also holds that the sculptor had to work very rapidly to complete its feature and make it perfect. A shrine to Bhogar exists in the southwestern corridor of the temple, which, by legend, is said to be connected by a tunnel to a cave in the heart of the hill, where Bhogar continues to meditate and maintain his vigil, with eight idols of Murugan.

The deity, after centuries of worship, fell into neglect and was suffered to be engulfed by the forest. One night, Perumal, a king of the Chera Dynasty, who controlled the area between the second and fifth centuries A.D., wandered from his hunting party and was forced to take refuge at the foot of the hill. It so happened that Subrahmanyan (Lord Murugan), appeared to him in a dream, and ordered him to restore the idol to its former state. The king commenced a search for the idol, and finding it, constructed the temple that now houses it, and re-instituted its worship. This is commemorated by a small stela at the foot of the staircase that winds up the hill.

As per Hindu legendary beliefs, Sage Narada visited the celestial court of Shiva at Mount Kailash to present him a fruit, the gnana-palam (literally, the fruit of knowledge). He decided to award it to whichever of his two sons who first encircle the world thrice. Accepting the challenge, Murugan (Kartikeya) started his journey around the globe on his mount peacock. However, Ganesha, who surmised that the world was no more than his parents Shiva and Shakti combined, circumambulated them and won the fruit. Murugan was furious and felt the need to get matured from boyhood and hence chose to remain as a hermit in Palani. The idol of the deity is said to be made of an amalgam of nine poisonous substances which forms an eternal medicine when mixed in a certain proportion. It is placed upon a pedestal of stone, with an archway framing it and represents the god Subrahmanya in the form he assumed at Palani - that of a very young recluse, shorn of his locks and all his finery, and dressed in no more than a loincloth and armed only with a staff, the dhandam, as befits a monk.

The temple is situated upon the higher of the two hills of Palani, known as the Sivagiri. Traditionally, access to it was by the main staircase cut into the hill-side or by the yanai-padhai or elephant's path, used by the ceremonial elephants. Pilgrims bearing water for the ritual bathing of the idol, and the priests, would use another way also carved into the hill-side but on the opposite side. Over the past half-century, three funicular railway tracks have been laid up the hill for the convenience of the pilgrims, and supplemented by a rope-way within the past decade. There are two modes of transport from the foothills to uphill. There is a winch, which operate from 6 a.m. on ordinary days and 4 a.m. during festive occasions. There is another rope car which operates from 7 a.m. to 12:30 p.m. and 1:30 p.m. to 5 p.m. Both winch and the rope car are closed after the Irakkala Pooja at 8 p.m. As of 2016, the temple was the richest among temples in the state with a collection of 33 crore during the period of July 2015 to June 2016. Palani temple is considered synonymous with Panchamritam, a sweet mixture made of five ingredients, and offered as 'prasadam' to devotees.

Famous Temples in Tamil Nadu

13. SOUNDARARAJA PERUMAL TEMPLE, THADIKOMBU

The Soundararaja Perumal temple in Thadikombu, a beautiful village 10 km south of Dindigul, is considered to be as sacred as the Kallazhagar temple near Madurai. Arulmighu Soundararaja Perumal is found in the sleeping posture in this temple and it is said that this place was previously known as Thaalamaapuri. Though it is a Vaishnava temple, the sthalavriksha here is the vilva tree (Wood-Apple in English, Bael in Hindi), usually associated with Lord Shiva.

Legend has it that near the river Kudaganaru, the sage Mandugar was doing penance. Thalaasuran, a demon, tried to spoil the sage's efforts. Lord Azhagar from Thirumaliruncholai (Azhagar temple) destroyed the demon and protected the sage's penance. The sage prayed to the Lord to stay and bless the devotees and so Azhagar gives darshan as Soundaraja Perumal in this temple. This temple is supposed to be as important as the Azhagar temple near Madurai and history states that it was built 500 years ago by Achutha Devarayar of the Vijayanagar Empire.

There is an idol of Hayagriva, who is believed to bestow good education on devotees, in this temple where vows that have to be fulfilled in Azhagarkoil can be fulfilled.

The sculptures in this temple speak of the artistic skill of the builders and it is surprising to see even minute details like the nail tip, muscles, nerves and eyelashes sculpted with such finesse. Chithirai Tiruvizha is celebrated for five days in an elaborate manner and thousands participate in the ten-day Aadi-Pournami Peruntiruvizha.

The temple is noted for its sculptures of rare and minute workmanship. The temple may well be called a treasure house of Indian sculptures of rare workmanship which speak volumes. Mother Soundaravalli graces in a separate shrine. Lord Vinayaka, Vishnu, Durga and deities of prosperity, Sanganidhi and Padmanidhi graces at her shrine. Mother's shrine may well be called a museum of sculptures. The sculptures include Lord Vishnu measuring the three worlds, Lord Narasimha, Vaikundanathar, Venugopala, Lord Vishnu on Gaurda, Anjaneya carrying Lord Rama on his shoulders, Chakarathalwar, Oordhvathandavar (cosmic dance of Lord Shiva), Oordhvakali, Akora Veerabadra, Rathi and Karthaveeryarjuna.

Lord Soundararaja Perumal graces from sanctum sanctorum with his consorts Sridevi and Bhudevi in a standing form. As it is believed that Lord Kallazhagar of Madurai has connections with this place also, a festival of the Lord visiting the Kudaganaru River is celebrated as in Madurai in Vaigai River. The festival represents the grace of the Lord to Sage Mandukya. On each

Tiruvonam star day, a dheep is lit at the feet of the Lord. The procession deity would be following the lamp taken before Him. It is believed that those fortunate to have this darshan would be relieved of their sins. The Swarna Aakarsha Bairavar here is believed to solve people's economic problems.

Famous Temples in Tamil Nadu

14. MEENAKSHI AMMAN THIRUKKOIL, MADURAI

Meenakshi Amman temple, also known as Meenakshi-Sundareshwara temple, is one of the oldest and most important temples in India. Located in the city of Madurai, the temple has a great mythological and historical significance. It is believed that Lord Shiva assumed the form of Sundareswarar (the handsome one) and married Parvati (Meenakshi) at the site where the temple is currently located. Renowned for its astonishing architecture, Meenakshi temple was nominated as one of the wonders of the world, but couldn't make it into the list of 'Seven Wonders of the

World'. However, the temple is definitely one of the 'Wonders of India'. It is also one of the main attractions of South India with thousands of devotees thronging it every day. During the 'Tirukalyanam Festival', which takes place over a period of 10 days, the temple attracts more than a million devotees. Despite many people visiting it every day, the temple is well-maintained and was named the 'Best Swachh Iconic Place' (cleanest iconic place) in India.

The history of Meenakshi temple dates back to the 1st century C.E with scholars claiming it to be as old as the city itself. It is said that Kulashekarar Pandyan, a king who ruled over the Pandyan dynasty, built the temple as per the instructions given in his dream by Lord Shiva. A few religious texts that belong to the 1st to 4th century C.E talk about the temple and describe it as the central structure of the city. Texts dating back to the early 6th century, describe the temple as a place where scholars met to discuss important topics. The temple as it stands today, however, was rebuilt throughout the 16th century after it was destroyed by the Muslim invaders.

During the 14th century C.E, Malik Kafur, a commander of Delhi Sultanate, led his army into the most parts of southern India and looted many temples including the famed Meenakshi temple. Valuables, such as gold, silver and precious gems were taken to Delhi. Since temples in those days had abundance of valuables, most of the temples were destroyed and were left in ruins. When the Vijayanagar Empire took over Madurai after defeating the Muslim Sultanate, the temple was rebuilt and reopened. The temple was further expanded during the late 16th century and early 17th century by Vishwanatha Nayakar, a king of the Nayaka dynasty. According to researchers, while rebuilding the temple, the rulers of Nayaka dynasty followed the architectural style of 'Silpa-Shastras'. 'Silpa Shastras' are a set of architectural laws found in the ancient texts. According to a legend, Meenakshi emerged out of a 'Yajna' (sacred fire) as a three-year-old girl. The 'Yajna' was performed by a king named Malayadwaja Pandya along with his wife Kanchanamalai. Since the royal couple had no child, the King offered his prayers to Lord Shiva, requesting him to grant them a son. But to their dismay, a triple-breasted girl emerged from the sacred fire. When Malayadwaja and his wife expressed their concern over the girl's abnormal appearance, a divine voice ordered them not to fret over the girl's physical appearance. They were also informed that the girl's third breast will disappear as soon as she meets her future husband. The relieved King named her Meenakshi and in due course crowned her as his successor.

The temple was once again expanded by Thirumalai Nayak who ruled over Madurai from 1623 to 1655. During his reign, many 'Mandapams' (pillared halls) were built. The temple was then expanded by many later Nayaka rulers before the advent of the British East India Company. The temple was once again degraded and parts of it were destroyed during the British Rule. In 1959, the restoration work was started by Tamil Hindus by collecting donations and by collaborating with historians and engineers. The temple was completely restored in 1995.

Meenakshi ruled over the ancient city of Madurai and also went on to capture the neighboring kingdoms. Legend has it that she even captured Indralok, the abode of Lord Indra, and was on her way to capture Kailash, the abode of Lord Shiva, as well. When Shiva appeared before her, Meenakshi's third breast disappeared and she knew that she had met her better half. Shiva and Meenakshi returned to Madurai where their wedding took place. It is said that the wedding was attended by all the gods and goddesses. Since Parvati herself had assumed the form of Meenakshi, Lord Vishnu, Parvati's brother, handed her over to Lord Shiva. Even today, the wedding ceremony is celebrated every year as 'ChithiraiThiruvizha' which is also known as 'Tirukalyanam' (the grand wedding).

The temple occupies a huge area in the heart of Madurai as it spreads over 14 acres. The temple is enclosed with huge walls, which were built in response to the invasions. The entire structure, when viewed from above, represents a mandala. A mandala is a structure built according to the laws of symmetry and loci. The temple is known as Velliambalam or the hall of silver to distinguish it from Ponnambalam the hall of gold, of the Chidambaram temple. The walls of the temple enclose a rectangular space that is 830 ft by 730 ft. There are various shrines built within the temple complex. Apart from the two main shrines, which are dedicated to Sundareswarar and Meenakshi, the temple has shrines dedicated to various other deities like Ganesha and Murugan. The temple also houses goddesses Lakshmi, Rukmini, and Saraswati.

The temple also has a consecrated pond named 'Porthamarai Kulam'. The term 'Potramarai Kulam' is a literal translation of 'pond with a golden lotus'. The structure of a golden lotus is placed at the center of the pond. It is said that Lord Shiva blessed this pond and declared that no marine life would grow in it. Sage Agastya said that the water of this tank was the holiest in the world. The area around this tank was the meeting place of the Tamil sangham – the ancient academy of poets. The history of the sangam goes back to the days when gods dallied with men. This academy judged the worth of any work of literature presented before it by throwing it into the tank. Only those that did not sink were considered worthy of attention.

The temple has four main towering gateways (gopurams) that look identical to each other. Apart from the four 'gopurams', the temple also houses many other 'gopurams' that serve as gateways to a number of shrines. The temple has a total of 14 towering gateways. Each one of them is a multi-storey structure and displays thousands of mythological stories and several other sculptures. The details of the four outer Gopurams are as follows:

i. East Tower (Nine Storeys). Height 161'3″. This tower has 1011 sudhai figures.

ii. South Tower (Nine Storeys). Height 170'6". This tower has 1511 sudhai figures.

iii. West Tower (Nine Storeys). Height 163'3". This tower has 1124 sudhai figures.

iv. North Tower (Nine Storeys). Height 160'6". This tower has fewer figures of sudhai than other outer towers.

The "Ayiramkaal Mandapam" or the Hall of Thousand Pillars is an architectural masterpiece. Though popularly called the 1000-pillared hall the actual number of pillars is 985. Each pillar is intricately carved and features huge, ornate and bold sculptures that are lifelike. Viewed from any angle these pillars are found to be in a straight line. In the outermost corridors are situated the matchless musical pillars (part of a single stone column) carved in stone. When they are tapped, though made of a single stone each pillar produces a different musical note. A Temple Art Museum is now housed in the 1000 pillars hall where one can see icons, photographs, drawings, etc., chronicling the 1200 year history of the city. There are so many other smaller and bigger Mandapams in the temple.

Since Meenakshi is the main deity of the temple, the temple signifies the importance of woman in a Tamil Hindu family. The temple also portrays the cordial relationship between Shaivism, Vaishnavism and Shaktism. The Sundareswarar shrine is known as one fifth of 'Pancha Sabhai' (five courts) where Lord Shiva is believed to have performed the cosmic dance. Worship mainly involves rituals and processions. One of the rituals involves placing an image of Sundareswarar inside a palanquin which is then moved to the shrine of Meenakshi. The palanquin is taken into the shrine every night and is brought back to the shrine of Sundareswarar every morning. The devotees usually worship Meenakshi before offering their prayers to Sundareswarar.

15. BRIHADEESWARAR TEMPLE, THANJAVUR

Brihadeeshwara temple (Peruvudaiyar Kovil) is a Hindu temple dedicated to Shiva located in Thanjavur in the Indian state of Tamil Nadu. It is also known as Periya Kovil, Raja Rajeswara temple and Rajarajesvaram. It is one of the largest temples in India and is an example of Dravidian architecture during the Cholas period. Built by emperor Raja Raja Chola I and completed in 1010 AD, the temple turned 1000 years old in 2010. The temple is part of the UNESCO World Heritage Site known as the "Great Living Chola Temples", with the other two being the Gangaikonda Cholapuram and Airavatesvara temple.

The temple stands amidst fortified walls that were probably added in the 16th century. The vimanam (temple tower) is 216 ft

(66 m) high and is the tallest in the world. The Kumbam (the apex or the bulbous structure on the top) of the temple was for long believed to be carved out of a single rock, but now it is believed that it is made out of eight pieces of rocks spliced together, and weighs around 80 tons. There is a big statue of Nandi (sacred bull), carved out of a single rock measuring about 16 ft (4.9 m) long and 13 ft (4.0 m) high at the entrance. The original Nandi statue, carved during Raja Raja Chola's time, was replaced by later rulers and the original Nandi statue can still be seen at the Pragaram. The entire temple structure is made out of granite, the nearest sources of which are about 60 km to the west of temple. The temple is one of the most visited tourist attractions in Tamil Nadu.

Arulmozhivarman, a Tamil emperor who was popular as Raja Raja Chola I laid out foundations of Brihadeeswarar temple during 1002 CE. It was first among other great building projects by the medieval Cholas of Tamil Nadu. A symmetrical and axial geometry rules layout of this temple. Temples from same period and two following centuries are expressions of Tamils Chola power, artistic expertise and wealth. Emergence of these types of features, such as multifaceted columns along with projecting signals of square capitals signifies arrival of Chola style, which was new at that time.

It is one architectural exemplar, which showcases true form of Dravida kind of architecture in temples and is a representative of ideology of Chola Empire and Southern India's Tamil civilization. Brihadeeswarar Temple "testifies to Chola's brilliant achievements in architecture, painting, bronze casting and sculpture".

The inscriptions and frescoes on the walls of Brihadeeswarar temple record the rise and fall of the city's fortunes. Lord Shiva's representation is as a gigantic stone lingam. This is covered by a vimanam that extends to 216 feet. It is built with stones that are bonded and notched without any mortar. The topmost stone, an engineering marvel, weighs about eighty tons.

Raja Raja-I named this temple as Rajarajesvaram and the deity Shiva in Linga form as Peruvudaiyar, the temple is also known in the deity's name as Peruvudaiyar kovil (in Tamil language). In later period Maratta and Nayaks rulers constructed various shrines and gopurams of the temple.

The Brihadeeswarar Temple was completed in around 1010 in the southeastern part of the new capital Thanjavur constructed in the basin of the Kaveri (Cauvery) river by the king of the Chola Dynasty, Raja Raja I (r. 985-1014). It has also been called Rajarajesvara Temple after the king's name. It is one of the two greatest temples from the age of the Chola Dynasty together with the Rajendra-Cholisvara Temple built in the next new capital, Gangaikondacholapuram, which was constructed by his successor Rajendra I. Those constructions were prodigious national projects showing the Chola Empire's hegemony in south India.

It is said that the Brihadeeswarar Temple was erected in only seven years. Its precincts are surrounded with cloisters covering an area of 120 m by 240 m and are also surrounded outside with heavy brick walls for an area of 350 m square including a large tank (reservoir).

There is a Nandi Shrine, two continuous extensive Mandapas (worship rooms), an Antarala (antechamber), and a Vimana with a high tower, all in line on the east-west axis. On the same axis stand Gopurams (temple gateways) of the early phase at the eastern center of the cloister and the brick wall. They are the sole entrance spots to the temple precincts.

Though they are embellished with sculptures, they look much lower than later Gopurams of huge temples in south India, as the height of the Vimana is great in contrast. The second Gopura on the line of the cloisters is 24 m in both width and height, lower than the first Gopura, but its sculptures are larger, with a pair of Dvarapalas (guardian figures) on both sides of the doorway.

In the cloisters surrounding the precincts is a line of Lingas (phalluses), symbols of Shiva, and wall paintings from the Nayaka period on the rear walls delight the eye of pilgrims. This Brihadeeswarar temple made of granite and brick is the greatest work of the Dravidian (northern) style in its grand scale and high degree of perfection, alongside of the great temple in Gangaikondacholapuram. The development of stone temples in the southern Indian style, having started at the small temples at Mahabalipuram, reached their summit here. It became the model of the temples to be built in south India and Southeast Asia in the period of the Chola Dynasty.

However, after the end of the Chola Dynasty in the 13th century, temple style would change dramatically. Huge Vimanas would not be built anymore, rather temple precincts would be expanded, surrounding the temple in fold upon fold, and constructing only Gopurams in a colossal scale on the four sides. The outer Gopurams would be erected higher, and would eventually attain more than 60 m. The relationship of height between the main shrine and its gates would be completely reversed. From this point too, the Brihadeeswarar temple in Thanjavur is the best representative of orthodox south Indian temple architecture. Thanjavur Periya Koil is the grandest creation of Cholas and it is visible from any area in Thanjavur, perhaps the only temple with such a characteristic.

16. SRIVILLIPUTHUR ANDAL TEMPLE

As per a Hindu legend, Bhagavan Sriman Narayanan during his Varaha Avataram slayed an asuran called Kalinemi and took rest under the foot of a Banyan tree, along with his consorts Sri Mahalakshmi and Sri Bhooma Devi in a place called Shenbagaranyam (meaning beautiful forest, in Tamil). Shenbagaranyam was a small part of a large kingdom ruled by a queen, Malli, whose sons Villi and Puttan were hunters and used to hunt animals in Shenbagaranyam. One day these two hunters,

Villi and Puttan, went to the forest for hunting and spotted a tiger. They tried to kill the tiger with Puttan vigorously chasing it, while Villi lost track of his brother. However after some time the tiger managed to kill Puttan by hiding behind a tree and pouncing on him at an opportune time. Villi came searching for Puttan and on seeing his dead body was overcome with grief. After some time he fell asleep. During his sleep he had a dream. Sriman Narayanan along with his consort appeared in his dream and said, "O Villi do not grieve. We will get back your brother's life." He then mentioned about his previous appearance as vatapatrasayi in sayana thirukolam under the foot of the banyan tree and said that there was a cave near a huge banyan tree where his moorthy (statue) had been lying for a long time. There were also lots of gold coins and jewels near that place. He then instructed Villi to use the money in deforesting the place and building a village with a temple after installing the statue in the temple. Villi woke up to find his brother Puttan also alive and narrated his dream to Puttan. He then built a small town and a temple by installing the statue of the lord and thus the Vatapatrasayi temple was built. As a forest full of snake mounds was converted into a town by Villi it came to be known as Villiputhoor. Later with the advent of Sri Andal it got the name Srivilliputtur. Srivilliputtur is known by other names such as Varahakshetram, Thenpuduvai, Vadeswarapuram, Vadamahadamapuram, Shenbagaranyakshetram, Vikramacholachaturvedhimangalam, and Sridhanvipuri.

Srivilliputhur Andal temple is in Srivilliputhur, a town in Virudhunagar district in the South Indian state of Tamil Nadu, and is dedicated to the Hindu God Vishnu. Constructed in the Dravidian style of architecture by Periyazhvar with the prize money he obtained from religious debates in the court of Vallaba Pandya in Madurai, the temple is glorified in the Divya Prabandha, the early medieval Tamil canon of the Azhwar saints from the 6th–9th centuries AD. It is one of the 108 Divyadesam dedicated to Vishnu, who is worshipped as Vatapatrasayi and his consort Lakshmi as Andal.

Srivilliputtoor is synonymous with the saint-poetess Andal. But many may not be aware that the Andal temple is a separate entity, which was built after her foster father, Periyazhwar's time, encompassing within it the house where Andal and Periyazhwar lived. According to historians, the Andal temple was built in 788 A.D. Pandya, Chozha, Vijayanagar and Nayak rulers and the Bana kings, who ruled with area around Azhagarkoil, near Madurai as their capital, later expanded it. The Nayak King, Thirumalai Nayak renovated all the temples of this city. He installed choultaries, temple tanks, paintings and golden towers inside the temple. The sculptures in the hall leading to the shrine of Andal were also built by him from 1751 to 1756 A.D. Then it fell into the hands of Mohammed Yousoof Khan. Until 1850, Sri Andal temple was under the care of the king of Travancore. The temple's gateway tower (Gopuram) is 192 ft (59 m) tall. It is generally held that this is the official symbol of the Government of Tamil Nadu (Sri Vatapatrasayi Temple Tower), but the subject is a matter of controversy as the artist who designed the emblem for the state of Tamil Nadu, Thiru Krishna Rao denied that it is not the temple of Srivilliputhur rather it is Meenakshi temple's West Gopuram.

The beautiful "Gopala Vilasam" in the front portion of the sanctum sanctorum, which is a rectangular hall, covered with wooden roof containing many sculpted images, and obtained from an ancient car of the temple, is not a general feature seen in other temples. It is here that the "Pahalpathu Adhyayana Uthsavam" is held in the Margazhi month. There is a golden Vimanam (dome) in this temple. This dome contains figures describing the songs of Thiruppavai, sung by Andal Herself.

Beautiful sculptural specimens adorn the pavillions of the temple. The various deities in the 108 Vishnu Shrines are also illustrated on the walls of the Temple.

Srivilliputtur finds mention in Brahmakaivatsapuranam and Varahapuranam. Varahapuranam foretells the existence of Srivilliputtur and the consequent visit of Vishnu during the Varaha Avataram. Brahmakaivatsapuranam mentions the location of Vatapatrasayi Temple in Srivilliputtur.

Srivilliputhur has a significant place in Vaishnava philosophy and worship practices. The Srivilliputtur divyadesam has the unique distinction among all other divyadesams of being the birthplace of two important azhwars among the twelve azhwars, sriperiyazhwar, who became the father-in-law of the Ranganatha himself and Andal who was the incarnation of Bhoomadevi and attained union with the Ranganathan at Srirangam. Andal is the only female Azhwar saint of the 12 Alvar saints of South India. She is credited with the Tamil works of Thirupavai and Nachiar Tirumozhi that are still recited by devotees during the winter festival season of Margazhi. The town-folk believe that waking up to the sounds of Thiruppavai is believed to lead to a sublime atmosphere throughout the day.

The temple follows Thenkalai tradition of worship. The temple priests perform the pooja (rituals) during festivals and on a daily basis. Like other Vishnu temples of Tamil Nadu, the priests belong to the Vaishnavaite community, a Brahmin sub-caste. The temple rituals are performed six times a day: Ushathkalam at 7 a.m., Kalasanthi at 8:00 a.m., Uchikalam at 12:00 p.m., Sayarakshai at 6:00 p.m., Irandamkalam at 7:00 p.m. and Ardha Jamam at 10:00 p.m. Each ritual has three steps: alangaram (decoration), neivethanam (food offering) and deepaaradanai (waving of lamps) for both Vatapatrasayi and Andal.

Before 2000, the practise of drawing the temple car during the yearly festival was suspended. With the efforts of Vanamamalai Jeeyar, the head of a monastic institution, the temple car was modified with hydraulic wheels to ease the movement. Kumbabishekam, the consecration of the Andal temple happened on 20th January 2016. Golden filials were also installed for Andal temple. A good time to visit temple are Fridays & Saturdays.

The temple is associated with the life of Andal, who was found under a Tulsi plant in the garden inside the temple by Periyalvar. She is believed to have worn the garland before dedicating it to the presiding deity of the temple. Periyazhvar, who later found it, was highly upset and stopped the practise. It is believed Vishnu appeared in his dream and asked him to dedicate the garland worn by Andal to him daily, which is a practise followed during the modern time.

17. SRI RANGANATHA SWAMY TEMPLE, TIRUCHIRAPALLI

Srirangam is the foremost of the eight self-manifested shrines (Swayam Vyakta Kshetras) of Lord Vishnu. It is also considered the first, foremost and the most important of the 108 main Vishnu temples (Divyadesams). This temple is also known as Thiruvaranga Tirupati, Periyakoil, Bhoologa Vaikundam, and Bhogamandabam. In the Vaishnava parlance the term "KOIL" signifies this temple only. The temple is enormous in size.

The temple complex is 156 acres in extent. It consists of seven Prakarams or enclosure walls, with streets and residences.

These enclosures are formed by thick and huge rampart walls which run round the sanctum. There are three circumambular streets known by different names, with high and majestic entrace-portals on the four sides of every street. There are several smaller shrines and mantapams within the enclosure, and of these, the Garuda Mantapam in the third enclosure and the Thousand Pillared Mantapam in the fourth are the grandest. There are 21 magnificent towers in all prakaras providing a unique sight to any visitor. The Vellai Gopuram (Literally, 'white entrance tower') of Sri Ranganathaswamy temple, Srirangam can be considered to be one of the finest Gopurams in South India. The proportions adopted in the construction of this gopuram indicate the intensive knowledge of the engineering aspect of this vast structure. Outside the temple, a road running along the southern, western and northern sides gives access to a large square lotus-covered tank, built not far from the western gopuram, and to the coconut plantations arid fields cultivated for the temple. This temple lies on an islet formed by the Twin Rivers Cauvery and Coleroon. The temple of Sri Ranganathaswami at Srirangam boasts an historic past of great kingdom and a civilization thousands of years old.

The temple of Srirangam is situated at 10 degrees 52'N and 78 degrees 42'E towards the southern tip of India on an Island formed by two arms of the river Cauvery. The temple covers a vast area of about 6,31,000 Sqm. (156 Acres). The temple consists of seven Concentric rectangular enclosures round the sanctum sanctorum. The temple of Srirangam is the only one in India with seven enclosures, a sacred symbolic number which for present day Vaishnava believers represents either the seven centers of Yoga, or a reference to the seven elements making up the human body, in the center of which dwells the soul.

Upto the tenth century, literary sources alone testify to the existence of Sri Ranganathaswamy temple, Srirangam. The references to the temple are found in the Silappadikaram, a Sangam work, in the collection, "The Four Thousand Hymns" (Nalayirappirabandagal, or more simply Nalayiram, "The Four Thousand"). They describe the God of Srirangam, Vishnu, reposing on the couch of the thousand hooded serpent, as Ranganatha in its southern form, or as the Seshasayanamurti or the Anantasayana of Vishnu-Narayana of classifical northern Vishnuism; a cosmic God who is one of the specific figures of the cult of Vaishanava Bhakti, a concept which dates back to the Rig Veda. It was during the Fifteenth and Sixteenth centuries that the temple of Srirangam took on the appearance it has today. The vimana was rebuilt and gilded over, a new statue of the bird Garuda, in copper, replaced the one destroyed during the Muslim invasions, and was ceremoniously installed before the sanctuary in 1415. Many sanctuaries were restored, gopuras rebuilt, and the flagstaff of the temple (dvajastambha) was covered with 102 gold plates. Some of the gates as well as the Mukhamandapam (1526) were gold-placed. Cows, gardens, villages, large sums of money, gold, and gold objects used in worship were donated to the Temple. Between 1424 and 1429, plates, a pedestal for the goddess, a sanctuary lamp (dipika), a vase (kalasa) and a garment of pearls were also received by the temple. It has withstood a lot of natural disasters as well. The site was fortified and expanded with many more gopurams in the 16th and 17th centuries.

Ranganathaswamy temple is the only one out of the 108 temples that was sung in praise by all the Azhwars (Divine saints of Tamil Bhakthi movement), having a total of 247 pasurams (divine hymns) against its name. Acharyas (guru) of all schools of thought – Advaita, Vishistadvaita and Dvaita recognise the immense significance of the temple, regardless of their affiliations. Nalayira Divya Prabhandam is a collection of 4000 hymns sung by twelve azhwars saints spread over 300 years (from the late 6th to 9th century AD) and collected by Nathamuni (910–990 AD). Divya Desams refer to 108 Vishnu temples that are mentioned in Nalayira Divya Prabandham. 105 of these are located in India, 1 in Nepal, while 2 are located outside of the Earthly realms. Divya in Tamil language indicates premium and Desam indicates place or temple. Periyazhvar begins the decade on Srirangam with two puranic stories according to which Krishna restored to life the son of his guru Sandeepani and the children of a Brahmin. Thondaradippodi Azhvar and Thiruppaana Azhvar have sung exclusively on Ranganatha. Andal attained Sri Ranganatha on completion of her Thiruppavai (a composition of 30 verses) in Srirangam. In total there are 247 hymns of the 4000 Pasurams dedicated to Ranganthar deity of this temple. Except Madhurakavi Azhvar, all the other eleven azhwars have created Mangalasasanam (praise) about the Ranganathar in Srirangam. Out of 247, 35 are by Periyazhvar, 10 by Aandaal, 31 by Kulasekara Azhvar, 14 by Thirumalisai Azhvar, 55 by Thondaradippodi Azhvar, 10 by Thiruppaan Azhvar, 73 by Thirumangai Azhvar, one by Poigai Azhvar, 4 by Bhoothathazhvar, two by Peyazhvar and twelve by Nammazhvar. Kulasekarar (Cheraman II) gave up his kingdom to his son during 798 AD and started visiting temples and singing praises about them. He visited the temple, praised the presiding deity and his works are compiled in Nalayira Divya Prabandam.

Throughout the day, pujas are performed; the morning one being the most important. The Temple follows a schedule which is virtually unchanged since ancient times and it'is practically the same in all the temples dedicated to Vishnu. It begins with the Brahmans serving in the holy of holies (Bhagavata-Nambis or Bhattal) washing symbolically the God's teeth, hands and feet. A servant holds a mirror before the Deity's visage.

An ablution is arranged for the Image of God with hot water; He is then anointed with ghee 0 and dried with saffron powder. Sandal paste is applied to the Godly figure's breast and feet; on Fridays, during certain seasons, oil is mixed with camphor for the Holy Bath which is given either publicly or secretly in the sanctuary, depending on circumstances. The Sacred Figure is then clothed in clean dry garments and the sacred sign (Namara) applied to his forehead. Jewels and garlands of fresh decorate the Deity while the musicians provide enthralling music from veena. The curtain is thereafter raised for the devotees to have Darshan of the Holy Image for about an hour. Neivedyam means the offering of food to the Deity. These preparations are produced in the kitchens of the Temple. Quids '6f betel and areca-nut are then set before God. After this ritual, a mouth-washing takes place. There follow various offerings (incense, small butter lamps, leaves of basil or tulasi, flowers) accompanied by recitations. The ritual comes to a close after the devotees and their offerings are presented to the Holy Being.

Pagal Pathu (10 day time) and Ra Pathu (10 day night time) festival is celebrated in the month of Margazhi (December–January) for twenty days. The first ten days are referred as Pagal-Pathu (10-day time festival) and the second half as Ra Pathu (10 day night-time festival). The first day of Ra Pathu is Vaikunta Ekadashi. The eleventh day of each fortnight in Hindu calendar is called ekadasi and the holiest of all ekadasis as per vaishnavite tradition is the Vaikunta Ekadashi. During the festival, through song and dance, this place is affirmed to be Bhooloka Vaikuntam (Heaven on Earth). Araiyar Sevai is a divine colloquim of araiyars, who recite and enact Nalayara Divya Prabanda, the 4000 verses of Azhvars. Araiyars are born to Araiyar tradition most prevalent in Sri Vaishnava families in Srirangam, Azhwar Thirunagari and Srivilliputhur.

The tradition of Araiyar Sevai was started by Nathamuni during 10th century. It is believed as per Hindu mythology that 33 crores of gods come down to witness the event. The processional deity is brought to the 1000-pillared hall on the morning of Vaikunta Ekadashi through the Paramapada Vasal (gate to paradise). Lakhs of pilgrims rush to enter it after the gate is opened and the deity passes through it as it is believed that one who enters here will reach vaikuntam (heaven) after death. The gate is open only during the ten days of Ra Pathu (10-day night-time festival). On the last day of the festival, the poet Nammazhwar is said to be given salvation. The performance is enacted by priests and images in the temple depicts Nammazhwar as reaching heaven and getting liberation from the cycle of life and death. At that point, a member from the crowd of devotees, who are witnessing this passion play, goes up to the centre stage and requests Vishnu to return Nammazhwar to humanity, so that his words and form in the temple will continue to inspire and save the devotees. Following this performance of the salvation of Nammazhwar, the cantors are taken in procession round the temple. Srirangapattana has mystical powers and immensely popular beliefs in God and the supernatural. It is believed that one who prays in all these three temples in a single day will attain Moksha or escape from rebirth.

18. JAMBUKESWARAR TEMPLE THIRUVANAIKAVAL TRICHY

Jambukeswarar temple, Thiruvanaikaval (also Thiruvanaikal, Jambukeswaram) is a famous Shiva temple in Tiruchirapalli (Trichy) district, in the state of Tamil Nadu. The temple was built by Kocengannan (Kochenga Chola), one of the Early Cholas, around 1,800 years ago. It is located in the Srirangam Island, which has the famous Ranganathaswamy temple.

Thiruvanaikal is one of the five major Shiva temples of Tamil Nadu (Pancha Bhoota Sthalam) representing the Mahābhūta or five great elements; this temple represents the element of water, or neer in Tamil. The sanctum of Jambukeswara has an underground water stream and in spite of pumping water out, it is always filled with water. It is one of the 275 Paadal Petra Sthalams, where all the four most revered Nayanars (Saivite Saints) have sung glories of the deity in this temple. The temple has inscriptions from the Chola period.

As an Elephant was blessed here after worshipping here, this temple came to be known as 'Thiruvanaikkaval' (Aanai/Yanai means Elephant in Tamil). As Lord Shiva is seated below the Jambu tree at this temple, it got its name Jambukeswaram. When Goddess Ahilandeswari penanced here, Lord Shiva, satisfied by her prayer, blessed her. For this reason this temple is also known as Gnanashethram.

A spider, which worshipped Lord Jambukeswarar in its previous life, was blessed to born as Kochengatcholan in its next birth. He constructed this temple about 2500 years ago. Legends have it that Uma Deviyar, Thirumal, Brahman, Attathikku Balakhar, Attavasukkal, Jambu Munivar, Gowthamar, Aghasthiyar, a spider known as Gananatharulmaliyavan, an elephant named Pushbadhanthan, Suryan and Chandran attained glory by worshipping at this temple.

Monolithic stone pillars (made from single stone) are found in the mandapam, situated at the entrance of Aariyavittan tower in 3rd Praharam. Stone chains and 12 zodiac signs are beautifully carved on these pillars. Pillars found in 1000 pillar hall and in various parts of temple have artistic sculptural works. In the year 1910, 2 big temple cars were made for god & goddess. 'Coratham' (used for procession) and several wooden Vahanas are present in this temple. Inscriptions of King Madurai-konda Parakesarivarmanparanthakacholan is the oldest among them. Information about renovations and wealth of this temple are found in these inscriptions.

The king who built the temple gave wages to his sculptors for building the fifth Prakara of the shrine by way of Vibhuti instead of gold coins. The entrance of the garbhagriha is so small that an elephant cannot enter inside. The Sthala Vriksha is Jamun tree. Like Meenakshi and Kamakshi temple Goddess Akhilandeshwari is famous in this temple.

Devotees believe that once, Devi Parvati made fun of Lord Shiva's penance for the improvement and welfare of the world. So, Lord Shiva asked her to go to the earth from Kailash (Lord Shiva's abode) to perform her penance.

Parvati in the form of Akilandeswari as per Shiva's wish found Jambu forest (Thiruvanaikoil) to conduct her penance. Hence, she made a lingam out of the water of river Cauvery under the Venn Naaval tree (the Venn Naaval tree on top of the saint Jambu) and commenced her worship. Threfore, the *lingam* is known as Appu Lingam (Water Lingam). Shiva at last gave darshan to Akilandeswari and taught her Shiva Gnana. Further, Akilandeswari took *Upadesa* (lessons) facing East from Shiva, who stood facing west.

Lord Shiva is the sole deity and also the temple has various mentions in many of the tales of Mahabharata and Lord Shiva. The God of this temple is called as the Destroyer and is also considered to be the most potent God of the Hindu trinity. One thousand eight names of the deity are known and are worshipped mainly as a lingam.

The priests of the temple follow many rituals while worshipping the deities at the temple. There are many minute details that are to be kept in mind while worshipping the main deity, Lord Shiva at the temple. And, because of which outsiders are not allowed inside the worshipping area during the ritual. The devotees are made to wait outside the temple and once the rituals are over, devotees can go inside and seek the blessing from Lord Shiva and offer Puja in their own way. Also, separate Aarti is performed for other two idols at the temple. Aarti is performed twice in the whole day, once in morning and once in the evening which is known as main aarti or Maha-aarti.

The five Shiva temples is referred to as Pancha Bhoota Sthalam and each of them represent the five prime elements of the nature that is air, water, space, Earth and fire. Here, Pancha refers to as five, Bhoota refers to as elements and Sthala is used for place. All these Pancha Bhoota temples are located in the South India, four of which are in Tamil Nadu and one in the state of Andhra Pradesh in India. It is believed that the five elements are enshrined in the five lingams. Each of these five Lingams has been given a different name based on which element they represent. In the Jambukeswarar temple, Shiva has believed to manifest the water, five of the elements and is known as Appu Lingam.

According to mythology, Goddess "Akilandeshwari" performed penance and made Shiva Linga from the Cauvery water and placed under the naval tree. Goddess Akilandeshwari took Upadesam (lessons) from Lord Shiva at this temple, so even today during noon, the chief priest of the temple disguise themselves as Goddess Akilandeshwari and perform pooja to Lord Shiva (guru) and also perform Ghopooja (the worship of cow).

Since Goddess Akilandeshwari and Lord Shiva share a teacher and student relationship and so there is no "Thirukalyanam" here. Another interesting fact about Goddess here is that Akilandeshwari transforms herself into "Lakshmi", "Saraswathi" as well as "Durga" every day, by being Lordess Lakshmi in the morning, Lordess Durga in the Noon & transforming into Lordess Saraswathi in the Evening.

Here is another story behind the history of this temple once a spider as well as an elephant both worshipped Lord Shiva. The spider develops a web every day to worship the God, unaware of it the elephant would clear the web every day, the angered spider once entered in the ear of the elephant which resulted in the death of both. The spider in its next birth was 'KochengotChola' and constructed 78 bigger temples including this. This temple is constructed in such a way that Elephant cannot witness Lord Jambukeswarar.

In this temple, as Akilandeswari worshipped Lord Shiva, even today, at noon, the Archakar (temple priest) dresses in a female attire and does Pooja to Jambukeswarar and a Ghopooja to black colored cow, called Karam Pasu. This uchikaalapooja is very famous and a lot of people visit every day. Annabhishekam to lingam (covering the lingam with cooked rice) is a daily ritual performed in the temple.

19. MARIAMMAN TEMPLE, SAMAYAPURAM

Samayapuram Mariamman temple is a Hindu temple in Samayapuram in Tiruchirappalli in Tamil Nadu, India. Tamil Country is also known for treating goddesses as relievers of distresses of devotees. Hence they give importance to Kali and Mariamman. The Samayapuram Mariamman temple is a popular one in this regard. The main deity, Samayapurathal or Mariamman, a form of supreme mother goddess Durga or Maha Kali or Aadi Shakthi, is made of sand and clay like many of the traditional Mariamman deities, and is considered to be a very powerful Goddess; and hence unlike many other Hindu deities there are no abhishekams conducted to the main deity, but instead the "abishekam" is done to the small stone deity in front of it. It is believed by the devotees that the Goddess has enormous powers over curing illnesses and hence, it is a ritual to buy small metallic replicas, made with silver or steel, of various body parts that need to be cured, and these are deposited in the donation box. The temple attracts thousands of devotees on Sundays, Tuesdays and Fridays, the holy days for Mariamman.

Samayapuram is the second wealthiest (in terms of cash flows) temple in Tamil Nadu after Palani. The history of the temple is not very clear. Samayapuram was once a provincial capital of the Hoysalas, and it was known as Kannanur. The remnants of the Hoysaleshwara temple, known for Hoysala Architecture, is left in a dilapidated condition even today. The Sthalapuranam of Samayapuram informs that the presiding deity was taken out from Srirangam and installed at Samayapuram. The primary deity was installed during the time of Chokkanatha Nayaka (1706-1732). Tamils are staunch in their belief that this deity will offer child if the parents offer sugarcane.

There is scant history of the period before that though it is believed that the locals worshipped the Goddess for many centuries before building the current temple. One legend says that the present deity was at the Ranganathaswamy temple at Srirangam, and one of chief priests of the temple believed that the idol caused him illness and hence asked it to be removed from the temple. It is a common belief in that part of the region that such local Gods have immense powers and they must always be satisfied by proper offerings and sacrifices. The idol was moved outside Srirangam, and later found by some of the passer by who built a temple named, the Kannanur Mariamman temple. During that period (around the 17th century CE), Trichi was ruled by the Vijayanagar kings and the area was used as an army base. It is believed that they made a commitment to build the temple if they win the war and after attaining success, they built a shrine for the Goddess. Originally it was under the management of the Thiruvanaikaval temple, a popular one in the region. Later, the control was split and currently Samayapuram is under an independent trust monitored by the Government of Tamil Nadu, which also monitors the annadanam distribution. The new urchavarpanchaloga idol was donated to the temple in the year 1991.

The temple conducts rituals for five times in a day regularly. The Puchoridal festival conducted during the last Sunday of the Tamil month Masi is a significant one. A thirteen-day festival is arranged from the first day of Chithrai. The Pancha Prakara Tiravila is conducted for 14 days from the first day of Vaikari. The Taipusam festival is conducted for 14 days during the Tamil month Thai. During the Adipusam festival the Amman of this temple receives gifts from the Srirangam temple. These facts stand to prove the cultural elements of the Tamil Country. To promote spiritualism, a school known as Tirumurai Training School is functioning where the teachers teach Devaram, Tiruvasagam and Nalairaya Divya Prabandam to the students.

Samayapuram is a significant symbol of the native culture in rural Tamil Nadu and there a number of unique practices concerning the Mariamman temples. Samayapuram has been used a model to describe rural folklore in a number of researches on sociology and religion. During festivals, it is not unusual to find people doing extreme things to make their bodies suffer as an act of sacrifice including, walking over a red-hot bed of charcoal and holding hot mud-vessel in bare hands. Mariamman temples also typically involve Samiyattam wherein through a devotee. Goddess Mariamman chooses to talk to help and bless the gathered devotees. The personality of the Goddess as well as the tremendous strain put on the body by the channelling (both physically and emotionally), maybe interpreted by non-believers as hysteria or hyper-excitement.

20. PANCHAVARNASWAMY TEMPLE, WORAIYUR

Panchavarnaswamy temple (Panjavarnaswamy/Panchavarneswarar temple) is a Hindu temple dedicated to Lord Shiva, located in Woraiyur, a suburb in the town of Tiruchirapalli in Tamil Nadu, India. Shiva is believed to portray five different colours (The five colours, white, black, red, yellow and green), giving the name of the presiding deity, Panchavarnaswamy. The lingam is called the Panchavarneswar because the lord manifests in five types during the worship at different times as given below:

Morning – Ratna Linga

Noon – Spadika (Crystal) Linga

Evening – Pon (Gold) Linga

Mudal Jamam – Vaira (Diamond) Linga

Ardha Jamam – Chittera Linga

Panchavarnaswamy is revered in the 7th century Tamil Saiva canonical work, the Tevaram, written by Tamil saint poets known as the nayanars and is, therefore, classified as a Paadal Petra Sthalam. It has several inscriptions dating back to the Chola period. The temple has six daily rituals at various times from 5:30 a.m. to 8 p.m., and three yearly festivals on its calendar. The annual Srivari Brahmotsavam (prime festival) is attended by hundreds of thousands of devotees from far and near. The temple is maintained and administered by the Hindu Religious and Endowment Board of the Government of Tamil Nadu.

As per Hindu legend, Shiva is believed to have appeared for sage Udanga in five different colours in five parts of the day. The temple is also called as "Tirumukeechwaram" or "Kozhi". The 7th century Saiva canonical work Tevaram by Tirugnanasambandar mentions the place as "Tirumukeechwaram". Nagaraja, the serpent king was carrying the images of five different Lingams, which all got merged into one as the presiding deity at this temple. The temple is believed to have been worshipped by Garuda, sage Kathiru and wife of sage Kashyapa.

Panchavarnaswamy temple complex has three prakarams (outer courtyard) and a five-tiered rajagopuram (gateway tower). The central shrine faces east and holds the image of Panchavarnaswamy (Shiva) in the form of lingam made of granite. The granite images of the deities Ganesha (son of Shiva and god of wisdom), Murugan (son of Shiva and god of war),

Nandi (the bull and transport of Shiva) and Navagraha (nine planetary deities) are located in the hall leading to the sanctum. As in other Shiva temples of Tamil Nadu, the first precinct or the walls around the sanctum of Panchavarnaswamy has images of Dakshinamurthy (Shiva as the Teacher), Durga (warrior-goddess) and Chandikeswarar (a saint and devotee of Shiva). The second precinct is surrounded by granite walls.

The temple has many interesting legends. One such is that when the Chola King Veeravathithan's elephant became uncontrollable, a cock suddenly appeared and disciplined the elephant and disappeared. There is a description of this legend in the temple panels. Incidentally the place where the temple is located is also called Kozhiyur (place of cock) and the Lord of the temple is also named after it. Another interesting

fact is that a cock suddenly appeared inside the temple one day, a few years ago, and since then it is staying there, without being disturbed by the temple activities.

Interestingly, this is probably the only temple in Tamil Nadu to have a bicyclist sculpted in one of its walls. The vehicle was possibly a novelty in Tiruchi of the 1920s, when the temple had been renovated. Perhaps the sculptor had seen someone on a cycle, was impressed by it and had recorded it forever on stone.

The temple priests perform the puja (rituals) during festivals and on a daily basis. Like other Shiva temples of Tamil Nadu, the priests belong to the shaiva community, an ancient branch of sanatan dharma that practices the worship of Lord Shiva as the supreme god. The temple rituals are performed six times a day.

21. THIRUKKOZHI - SRI AZHAGIYA MANAVALA PERUMAL TEMPLE, TRICHY

Azhagiya Manavalan Perumal temple (also called Thirukozhi or Nachiyar Koil) in Uraiyur, a suburb Tiruchirappalli in the South Indian state of Tamil Nadu, is dedicated to the Hindu god Vishnu. Constructed in the Dravidian style of architecture, the temple is glorified in the Divya Prabandha, the early medieval Tamil canon of the Alvar saints from the 6th-9th centuries AD. It is one of the 108 Divyadesams dedicated to Lord Vishnu, who is worshipped as Azhagiya Manavalan and his consort Lakshmi as Kamalavalli.

The temple is believed to have been built by the Medieval Cholas of the late 8th century AD, with later contributions made by Pandyas, Vijayanagar kings and Madurai Nayaks. Azhagiya Manavalan is believed to have appeared to Kamalavalli, the daughter of Chola king Nanda Cholan, in this place to marry her.

A granite wall surrounds the temple, enclosing all its shrines and bodies of water. The temple has a five-tiered rajagopuram, the temple's gateway tower. Six daily rituals and three yearly festivals are held at the temple, of which the chariot festival, celebrated during the Tamil month of Chittirai (March–April), is the most prominent. The temple is maintained and administered by the Hindu Religious and Endowment Board of the Government of Tamil Nadu.

Once upon a time, there was a discussion among the great rishis that among Trimuthies, who is the greatest. But in that discussion also, they could not come to a conclusion that who is great amongst the Trinity. Finally, all the rishis thought it would be helpful for them to find the answer for this if they could get the sugesstion from the great muni, Brighu. They all explained about the discussion they had among them and said he is the right person to find a solution for this and clear their doubts what was there in their minds. Brighu muni also accepted their words and told them he would give an answer that would clear all of their doubts.

First, he went to Kailasam where Lord Shiva and Goddess Parvathi reside. But, in the entrance itself, Brighu muni was stopped by the Dwara Balakaas as the residing deities are all alone and doesn't want them to get disturbed. As he got this kind of answer in Kailash, he thought he could not be the right person who might help his devotees as he was not easy to talk with. As he was disappointed by this experience, he then left to Sathya Lokam where Lord Brahma and Goddess Saraswathi reside. There also he could not meet Brahma devan and he was reminded of when he went to Kailasam.

Finally, he went to Sri Vaikuntam where Sriman Narayanan and Goddess Sri Lakshmi reside. As Brighu muni entered Vaikuntam, he was greeted in a good manner and this first action made him to think that Sriman Narayanan is the right person to whom all persons and rishis can seek help and can have a direct approach towards him. Sriman Narayanan offered him with the seat and did the Paadha Pooja for him. But, this action of Sri Vishnu made Sri Lakshmi to be embarrassed asked the lord not to touch his feet. This action of Sri Lakshmi made Brighu muni to get angry and cursed her that she would born in the world as an ordinary human. But, Sri Lakshmi felt very sad for the sabham (Shaap) she got from Brighu muni but Sriman Narayanan said that all the actions are happening according to their fates only and added that he will follow her soon to earth. At the same time in earth, a king named Dharma Varman lived in Kumbakonam, Chozha Naadu. Once he went out for hunting and found that some rishis were being distressed by demons and sought help from the king. Dharma Varman said that he will help them from the demons by killing them and he stayed in the forest for some time.

The King slayed the demons, but disclosed the fact that he had no children, which distressed him a lot. He sought the help of the rishis to be blessed with a child. So, to help the king, all the rishis did a Yagam to get a child for the king. At that time, an Asareeri stated that if he want to get a child he should pray towards Sri Lakshmi and as a result, Sri Lakshmi itself will born as a child to him. Hearing this, he started to pray towards Sri Lakshmi and finally, a female child was born to him and was kept a name as "Vara Lakshmi".

As the days went on, Dharma Varman started to seek a perfect groom for his daughter and announced a Swayamvaram for that. Lots of kings came for this and at the same time, Sriman

Narayanan also came there one among the grooms. In that hall, when Sri Lakshmi came, she had a look at all the members in the hall and at the same time, she also noticed Sriman Narayanan came there and went straight towards him without any delay and garlanded him. All the persons saw this wedding of Sri Vishnu and Sri Lakshmi and the king raised a temple for Sri Ranganathar in Kalyana Thirukkolam (literally 'wedding attire').

The Utsavam done here starts in Panguni month lasts for 10 days. On the first day of Panguni Uthiram, Sri Ranganathar comes from Sri Rangam and stays in Urayoor. And on Panguni Uthiram, he marries Kamalavalli Naachiyar and gives his Kalyana Kola Seva to his Bhakthas. There is no Utsavar found in this sthalam as Sri Ranganathar of Sri Rangam came here to marry Sri Lakshmi and the Utsavar of Sri Rangam is considered to be the Utsavar of this sthalam too. In this sthalam, Periya Pirattiyar is giving her seva in two different ways.

One is Irundhaseva and the other one is Kidanthaseva. Combining these both sevas, she is giving seva as "Urayum" (from sitting seva to sleeping seva) seva, this temple is called "ThiruUrayoor". There is no Brahmotsavam conducted in this divyadesam.

The temple is believed to be the birthplace of Thiruppaan Azhvar, one of the Azhvar saints belonging to the 6th-8th centuries. The Thayaar (mother goddess) of this Sthalam is Sri Kamalavalli Naachiyaar (Vaasakshmi) who is also known as "Uraiyur Valli". She is found in Sitting (Veetrirundha) Kolam facing North direction. The position of the Thaayar is similar to position of a Bride who sits along with the Groom during marriage. The above positions are called as "Thirukalyana Avasaram".

22. SHORE TEMPLE, MAHABALIPURAM

The Shore temple (built in 700–728 AD) is so named because it overlooks the shore of the Bay of Bengal. It is located in Mahabalipuram in Tamil Nadu. Mahabalipuram, also known as Mamallapuram is situated on the Coromandal coast, 58 kms to the south of Chennai. It was designated a world Heritage site by UNESCO IN 1984 for its standing range of monuments, dating from the 6th century to the 10th century A.D. It formally served as a major port on sea lanes stretching from imperial China to Rome. From the third, through the ninth century, the kings of Pallava dynasty controlled the region from Kanchipuram their capital city 60 km inland. Architectural remains at the site indicate that Mamallapuram also served as a major ceremonial centre and residence of Pallava king from the sixth century onwards, though coins from still earlier periods have been found in dunes along its shores.

It is a structural temple, built with blocks of granite, dating from the 8th century AD. At the time of its creation, the site was a busy port during the reign of Narasimhavarman II of the Pallava dynasty. It is one of the oldest structural (versus rock-cut) stone temples of South India. Shore temple is a complex of temples and shrines. Since times immemorial, Mahabalipuram has always been a city whose fame has spread far and wide as being a seat of religion, learning and an important port in the ancient world. Mahabalipuram is located in the Kanchipuram district of Tamil Nadu and is home to several architectural monuments built between the 7th and the 9th century.

Mahabalipuram was at the height of its splendour and glory during the reigns of Narasimhavarman and Rajsimhavarman, who played important roles in building the many magnificient temples in the city as Mahabalipuram was the second capital of the Pallava kings. Legend has it that Mahabalipuram was created when Lord Vishnu killed the cruel Mahabali after a fierce battle. Formerly known as Mamallapuram, the city was renamed to its present name during the reign of Narasimhavarman 1.

The shore temple at Mahabalipuram is a world heritage site as classified by UNESCO and is believed to be the only existing temple amongst the seven shore temples that were originally constructed. The temple bears exquisite designs and carvings and is supposed to be the forerunner of Dravidian architecture. Visitors to the temple are greeted by delicately carved dwarpalaks, who are said to stand in guard of the deity inside.

Arjuna's Penance: This magnificent carving is unique in the range of Indian art. The scene is generally taken to represent a story from the Mahabharata in which Arjuna, the epic hero, performed penance to please Lord Shiva and thus to obtain the Pasupata weapon from him. Two large boulders with a narrow fissure in between have been chosen to represent a series of rows of gods and goddesses like Chandra, Surya, pairs of Kinnaras and Siddhas, Gandharvas, Apsaras, etc., rushing towards a central point hear the cleft where a sage stands on his left foot deeply engaged in penance involving physical mortification. To his right is a four-armed Lord Shiva of majestic bearing carrying a trident in one of his hands and attended by dwarf ganas. Apart from the celestials there are hunters, sages, disciples and wild animals like the lion, tiger, elephant and boar. The group of elephants, so faithfully true to nature, are real masterpieces that enhance the charm of this wonderful carving. The young ones nestling in the space between the legs of the parent animal and playing with trunks show delightful delineation of life. The cleft is occupied by gracefully carved figures of Nagas and Nagis with hands in adoration. Another wonderful part of the temple is the Krishna Mandapam, which is one of the largest mandapams and is dedicated to Lord Krishna, the mentor and guide of the Pandavas. The inside of this mandapam is decorated with carvings that depict incidents from Lord Krishna's life.

The Varaha Mandapam lies beside the Arjuna penance and is dedicated to Lord Vishnu's Varaha incarnation. The northern wall portrays Lord Vishnu standing on one foot atop Naga, the snake king attempting to rescue Prithvi, the Goddess of earth. The entrance to this mandapam has two pillars engraved with two horned lions that stand guard at the door of the mandapam.

Shore temple is also acknowledged for being the first stone structure made by Pallavas. Before this, the monuments used to be carved out of the rocks or stones. Unlike other monuments of the region, Shore temple is a five-storied rock-cut structural temple. In southern India, this is one amongst the earliest and most important structural temples. The spire is extensively decorated with carvings and sculptures. In the recent years, a stone wall has been constructed to protect the shrine from further sea-erosion. Perched on a 50 feet square plinth, the pyramidal structure raises to the extent of 60 feet. Presenting a typical specimen of Dravidian temple architecture, Shore temple generates an exclusive combination of history and natural splendor. The temple was designed to grasp the first rays of the rising sun and to spotlight the waters after sunset. In the words of Percy Brown, Shore temple served as "a landmark by day and a beacon by night".

23. PANCHAVATI, PONDICHERRY

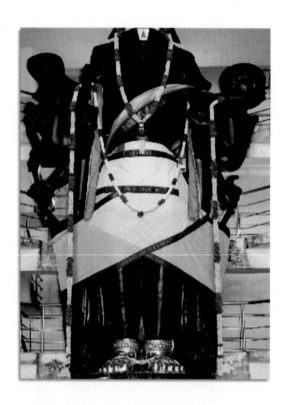

This stunning temple sprawls across 12 acres of land on the Pondicherry-Tindivanam road. Panchamuga Anjaneya Temple is located in Panchavati village, on the Pondicherry-Tindivanam Highway, in Villupuram district. The image of this Anjaneya (Hanuman) is 36 feet high and said to be one of the tallest Hanuman statues in India. The temple premises are very neat and well maintained. This famous Anjaneya temple is situated 12 km away from Pondicherry. This temple beams with the pride as it has the world's second largest Anjaneya effigy in the world. This temple is mostly crowded during Saturdays; some of the important festivals celebrated here are Krishna Jayanthi, and Vaikunta Ekadasi. Devotees offer Betel garland, butter and clothes to Anjaneya. They also prepare vada garland for the Lord which they later distribute to the poor people.

People suffering from incurable diseases and ceaseless struggles are advised to visit this temple for six consecutive Saturdays and chant the mantra of Jai Ram 108 times; they are also given a spiritual armlet.

The Pachamuga Anjaneya temple at Panchavatee/Panchvati is known for bestowing better health to the devotees. The idol is believed to have special powers and is considered a healer. The Temple has indeed become a landmark and no tourist bus in that route skips the Temple. The Temple is accessible by road NH 45A.

This vision of Pachamuga Anjaneya with five faces – his own in the centre, surrounded by Garuda, Hayagreeva, Narasimha and Varaha. Hayagreeva is the horse form of Lord Vishnu, Narasimha the lion and Varaha the boar.

Devotees throng this temple to offer Lord Anjaneya a garland of ulunduvadas, known popularly as Hanumarvadas. The significance behind offering ulunduvada is that ulundu has the property of cooling and is supposed to reduce Anjaneya's ugram and make him beneficent to his devotees. The other reason is that the vada has ingredients that will please Saneeswaran, Rahu and Ketu.

It is believed that devotees of Anjaneya do not get affected by planetary positions. On Saturdays, the day most auspicious for Saneeswaran, there are as many vadamalas which are offered to Anjaneya.

Famous Temples in Tamil Nadu

24. ARULMIGU MANAKKULA VINAYAGAR TEMPLE

The Manakkula Vinayagar temple is a Hindu temple in the Union Territory of Puducherry, India. Dedicated to Lord Ganesha, it is a popular pilgrimage site and tourist destination in Puducherry. The temple is of considerable antiquity and predates French occupation of the territory. During the tenure of Dupleix, there were attempts to destroy the temple, even the idol was displaced and thrown into the sea, but legends say that the idol would surface everytime; eventually, the temple was spared owing to strong protests from the Hindu population amidst the threat of British and Maratha invasion of the territory. The presiding deity was earlier known as 'vellakara (white man) Vinayagar', as this place was part of the town where French and white people lived.

This temple was built before the 15th century; the ancient Arulmigu Manakkula Vinayagar temple is located 400 metres away from the Bay of Bengal in White Town, Pondicherry. This shrine is dedicated to Bhavaneshar Ganapathy – a form of Lord Ganesha, who is known as the remover of obstacles. In Tamil, manal means sand and kulam means pond. When the temple was made, there was a pond full of sand close to it; hence, the name Manalkulam was given to the religious edifice.

This temple is spread over an area of 7913 sqft. This quaint shrine boasts a beautifully constructed mandapam, raja gopuram and prahara – the area where idols of other deities are placed. Measuring 18 feet in height, the gold plated kodikambam is a spectacular architectural highlight of this temple. The walls of this religious edifice have been decorated with intricate paintings that depict significant events from Hindu mythology. The rich architectural beauty of the shrine is enhanced by a golden vimanam and a golden kavasam.

The idol of Lord Ganesha – the main deity of this shrine rests on a golden chariot. The use of teak wood and gold racks gives an exquisite look to the chariot. You will be amazed to know that around 7.5 kilograms gold has been used in the making of the chariot. Every year during Dussehra, this chariot is carried out so that devotees can seek the blessings of Lord Ganesha on the day of Vijayadashmi.

Inside the temple, on the southern side pragaram wall three rows of sculptures of various gods and stone engravings are placed. In the top row 33 different types of Vinayagar idols and in the second row 25 types of Vinayagar idols; and in the third row stone engravings of Vinayagar Kavasam, Bharathiyar Vinayagar Nanmanimalai, Ashtalakshmisthothiram, Idumban & Kadamban Kavasam and Sri Vinayagar Asthothiram are found. The temple has some very fine paintings depicting the scenes of religious and historical significance. Some of them are the Birth of Lord Vinayagar, killing of Kayamuga Asura, Vinayagar marrying Suddhi and Buddhi, Vinayagar blessing Nambiyandar Nambi, etc.

An ancient story associated with the temple states that almost 300 years ago, a saint named Thollaikkathu Siddhar attained samadhi in the premises of this pious site. Since then, it is believed that bringing newborn babies to this shrine before taking them to any other shrine is auspicious. Many festivals are celebrated in this religious complex throughout the year. Brahmothsavam is one of the major annual festivals celebrated here (August and September). Devotees and tourists come here from all corners of the country to seek blessings of the deity and to admire the splendour of this prominent place of worship.

25. CHITHAMBARAM NADARAJAR TEMPLE

Chidambaram temple is a Hindu temple dedicated to Lord Shiva located in the heart of the temple town of Chidambaram, Tamil Nadu. The temple is located 78 km south of Pondicherry and 235 km from Chennai, the capital of Tamil Nadu state. The temple, known to be one of the oldest in South India, covers more than 40 acres and has four gopurams, the north and south ones towering to 49 m high. Two of the gopurams are carved with the 108 classical postures of Nataraja - Shiva in his role as the cosmic dancer. The features of the temple are the 1000-pillared hall, the Nritta Sabha court carved out like a gigantic chariot, the image of Nataraja himself in the inner sanctorum. An interesting feature of this temple is that unlike most temples dedicated to Shiva; this one represents Him as an idol instead of the customary lingam.

According to puranic version, Chidambaram is, otherwise, called as "Thillai" as the whole area was originally a Forest of Thillai (Coecaria Agallocha) shrubs and in which was found the Swayambu (natural) Sivalinga, the earliest object of worship of this great shrine. Lord Nataraja manifested his Cosmic dance (Aanandha Thandavam) at Thillai and wanted the offering of prayers by people so that he could continue this mystic dance forever at Chidambaram. The great Natarajar temple is located almost at the center of the city, and covers an area of about 40 acres. This temple is one of the very few places where the deities of the Hindu Trinities, Shiva, Vishnu and Brahma, (who is rarely worshipped) are worshiped in one complex.

Outside the temple, there are four car streets, each sixty feet wide. There are 5 sabhas (halls) in the temple namely; 1) The Chit Sabha: The Mystic hall is the inner-most portion of the temple. It is the holiest, also known as Chit-ambalam has in turn given its name to the temple, and to the town. This sabha is the 'sanctum sanctorum' of Nataraja, where Lord Nataraja is seen dancing, and to his left is the 'sanctum sanctorum' of Goddess Sivakamasundari. To his right is the Chidambaram Rahasyam, wherein there is no image or Linga but a semi circular arch or Prabha with a veil in front. The Prabha is marked by a string of golden vilwa (bael) leaves hung over it, the prabha revealing mere ethereal space- the invisible presence- the symbol of God. It is for the worship of Shiva in His akasic or Fomless form, invisible to human eyes. The gold Plate covered canopy of the Chit Sabha is a major point of attraction to tourist as well as Pilgrims. His worship is also associated with His form as the five elements: Earth, water, fire, air and sky. The other four places held sacred to such special worship in the form of elements being: Kanchi as Earth, Thiruvannamalai as Fire, Thiruvanaikka as Water, and Kalahasti as air. The other Four sabhas named as Kanaga Sabha which is frontal complement to the Chit Sabha. The third one is the Deva Sabha or Perambalam lies outside the central courtyard and in the third prakara to the east of Nataraja's sanctum sanctorum. The fourth one is the Nritta Sabha that is the hall of the dance in which Lord Nataraja performed the Dance to vanguish Goddess Kali. It is the most interesting and most artistic structure of the temple. It is a graceful mandapam of exquisite style, supported with 56 pillars about 8 feet high and most delicately carved from top to bottom. The fifth one is the Raja Sabha, and is called the Devasiriya Mandapam, the hall of state, thousand-pillared and 338 feet long by 197 feet wide. It is ascribed to Chola Kulottunga III (1178-1216) who built it for the purpose of St. Sekkizhar's inaugurating the Tirutthondar Puranam.

The famous Naatyanjali festival is also organized every year inside the Lord Nataraja's Temple during "Maha Sivarathiri". Senior dancers of aspirant entrants use to participate in this festival as an act of Homage to Lord Nataraja. Four Samaya Kuravas namely, Appar, Sambandar, Sundarar and Manickkavasagar entered into the temple through West, East, North and South respectively to worship Lord Shiva. Thevaram and Thiruvasagam called as Twelve Thirumuraigal was founded from this ancient town.

The towers of this magnificent temple have interesting history. The eastern Gopuram was built by Chola Kulottunga II (1133–1150), in the 12th century. It is being in the height of 135 feet. The side walls of this long entrance bear sculptures in dance poses (Bharata Natya) carved out in hard granite. They are 108 in number, this each panel which gives the name of each karanam or pose as found in the Natya Sashthra of Bharatha. The south gopuram was built by Kopperunjiga also known as 'Bharathana Vallan' (1243 AD). It is seen from inscriptions, that it was begun in 1237 AD and completed in 1240 AD while Pallava was independent. The West gopuram, which is called Sundarapandiyan gopuram was built by Jatavarman Sundara 1

(1231 AD–1268 AD). A Special feature of this gopuram is that the names of the minor deities found in the niches are carved in Granatha Characters. The North gopuram was built by Krishnadevaraya I (1506–1530 AD) of Vijayanagar in 1516 in the memory of his victory over the Kalinga country. It is 1571 feet above sea level, and about 140 feet above gound level. There is a portrait of Krishnadevaraya (the Tuluva dynasty) seen worshipping adhikramemdo Siva at the inner gate way.

Chidambaram Nataraja temple is said to be contemporaneous to the Srirangam Ranganathaswamy temple (as per some accounts, it is regarded as older than the Srirangam temple) with both having been built in the BC era.

The temple suffered extensive damage and destruction during invasions by the armies of Alauddin Khilji led by Malik Kafur between 1299–1330 AD, with the temples at Srirangam and Madurai also bearing the brunt of these attacks. It was subsequently repaired by various Pandya kings, later Pallavas like Kopperinjunga, by Vijayanagara kings including Krishna Deva Raya and the Nayakas of Thanjavur. But all said and done, its antiquity and origins, certainly date from between 750–600 BC, and the BC era Cholas (and Pandyas) during whose period it must have been constructed.

It is believed that this temple is located at the Center Point of the world's Magnetic Equator. Of the "Panchabootha" i.e. 5 temples, Chidambaram denotes the Skies, Kalahasthi denotes Wind, Kanchi Ekambareswar denotes land. All these 3 temples are located in a straight line at 79 degrees 41 minutes Longitude. This can be verified using Google. An amazing fact & astronomical miracle!

Chidambaram temple is based on the Human Body having 9 Entrances denoting 9 Entrances or Openings of the body. Temple roof is made of 21600 gold sheets which denote the

21600 breaths taken by a human being every day (15 × 60 × 24 = 21600). These 21600 gold sheets are fixed on the Gopuram using 72000 gold nails which denote the total no. of Nadis (Nerves) in the human body.

With nine gateways representing the nine orifices of the human body, the temple is one of the most unique abodes of Shiva, in that, it is the only temple where Lord Shiva is present in three forms. The first of course the most famous, the human form of Nataraja wherein He is performing a cosmic dance, the second is in the form of a "Linga" and the third is the invisible form. This is yet another distinctive feature of the temple, in that, there is a firm belief that Lord Shiva exists as an invisible space within the sanctum sanctorum. This has given rise to the secret of Chidambaram aka "Chidambara Rahasyam". The temple opens every day at dawn (4 am) and stays open till noon. The evening darshan can be had from 4.30 pm to 9 pm. The special Puja ceremony, held at 5 pm every Friday is truly spectacular with fire rituals and clashing of bells and drums.

Chidambaram Nataraja Swamy

□□□

REFERENCES

[1] Sivaramamurti. C: The Art of Ancient India, (1978, Abhinav Publications, New Delhi)

[2] Singh, Upinder: A History of Ancient and Medieval India : From the Stone Age to the 12th Century, (2008, Pearson Education India, New Delhi)

[3] Talbot, Cynthia: Pre-colonial India in Practice: Society, Region and Identity in Medieval Andhra, (2001, Oxford University Press, New York)

[4] Srinivas. K.R: Temples of South India (1984, Publications Division, Ministry of Information and Broadcasting, New Delhi)

[5] Rao Sreenivasa. S, Temple Architecture – Devalaya Vastu, Part I, (Suleka.com)

[6] Official website of the Kanchi Kamakshi Amman temple

[7] Suresh B.Pillai, Introduction to the Study of Temple Art, Equator and Meridian, Thanjavur, 1976

[8] N. Vanamamalai Pillai, op.cit

[9] Tiruvannamalai, (Manivasakar Pathippagam, Chennai, 2001) authored by V. Narayanaswamy

[10] A.T.M. Panneer Selvam's Tiruvannamalai Malaivala Mahimai (Tamil), (Sri Seshadri Swamigal Ashramam, Tiruvannamalai, 2009

[11] Ambujam Anantharaman's, Temples of South India, (EastWest Books (Madras) Pvt. Ltd, Chennai, 2006)

[12] Senthil Selvakumaran. M., and Chandravanan. C., Heritage of Chidambaranar District, Tirunelveli, 1994

[13] Srinivasan.C.R., Kancheepuram through ages

[14] Gopalakrishnan.M., Gazetteers of Tamilanadu state – Kancheepuram & Thiruvallur Districts

[15] The Visual Complexity in the Temple forms of Pallava Architecture, Ranganathan and Subbaiyan

[16] Dr.James Hastings, The Encyclopaedia Religion and Ethics, Vol.XI

[17] Sreethara Menon, A., A Survey of Kerala History, Kottayam, 1964

[18] Govindarasu. K.A, Alvar varalaru (second Book), Tirunelveli Soth India Siva Sidhantham Book Society Limited., Tirunelveli

[19] Kalyanan.G, Guide and History of Sri Andal Temple, Srivilliputtur, Arulmigu Nachiar Thirukkoil, Srivilliputtur

[20] Jeannine Auboyer, Sri Ranganathaswami' A Temple of Vishnu in Srirangam, Madras, India, Paris, June, 1969

[21] Samayapuram Mariamman Temple Talavanralaru, Temple publication, Samayapuram, 1982

[22] Panchavarneswarar Temple Notice Board , Uraiyur

[23] Paramasivanandham, A.M: Ancient Temples of Tamil Nadu (1981, Tamil Kalai Publishing House, Madras

[24]   Rao Gopinatha, Elements of Hindu Iconography, Vol. I, Part I (1993, Motilal Banarasi Dass Publishers Pvt. Ltd., Delhi

[25]   https://en.wikipedia.org/wiki/Kamakshi_Amman_Temple

[26]   http://www.kanchikamakshi.com/

[27]   https://temple.dinamalar.com/en/new_en.php?id=444

[28]   https://en.wikipedia.org/wiki/Ramanathaswamy_Temple

[29]   https://en.wikipedia.org/wiki/Tiruvannamalai

[30]   https://en.wikipedia.org/wiki/Thiruchendur_Murugan_temple

[31]   http://www.sriparthasarathytemple.tnhrce.in/

[32]   https://en.wikipedia.org/wiki/Parthasarathy_Temple,_Chennai

[33]   http://www.mylaikapaleeswarar.tnhrce.in/

[34]   https://en.wikipedia.org/wiki/Kapaleeshwarar_Temple

[35]   https://en.wikipedia.org/wiki/Kanchi_Kailasanathar_Temple

[36]   https://en.wikipedia.org/wiki/Nagaraja_Temple,_Nagercoil

[37]   https://en.wikipedia.org/wiki/Devi_Kanya_Kumari

[38]   https://en.wikipedia.org/wiki/Golden_Temple,_Sripuram

[39]   http://www.siruvapurimurugantemple.tnhrce.in/

[40]   https://en.wikipedia.org/wiki/Nataraja_Temple,_Chidambaram

[41]   https://en.wikipedia.org/wiki/Palani_Murugan_temple

[42] https://en.wikipedia.org/wiki/Soundararajaperumal_temple,_Thadikombu

[43] https://en.wikipedia.org/wiki/Meenakshi_Temple

[44] https://en.wikipedia.org/wiki/Brihadisvara_Temple,_Thanjavur

[45] https://en.wikipedia.org/wiki/Srivilliputhur_Andal_temple

[46] https://en.wikipedia.org/wiki/Ranganathaswamy_Temple,_Srirangam

[47] https://en.wikipedia.org/wiki/Jambukeswarar_Temple,_Thiruvanaikaval

[48] https://en.wikipedia.org/wiki/Samayapuram_Mariamman_Temple

[49] https://en.wikipedia.org/wiki/Panchavarnaswamy_Temple

[50] https://en.wikipedia.org/wiki/Azhagiya_Manavala_Perumal_Temple

[51] https://en.wikipedia.org/wiki/Shore_Temple

[52] https://www.tripadvisor.in/Attraction_Review-g659792-d15267936-Reviews   Panchavati_Anjaneya Pondicherry_Union_Territory_of_Pondicherry.html

[53] https://en.wikipedia.org/wiki/Manakula_Vinayagar_Temple

[54] https://www.thehindu.com/features/metroplus/bringing-the-past-to-the-present/article7310014.ece

---